Course Notes

CONTRACT LAW

rd

HODDER EDUCATION
AN HACHETTE UK COMPANY

COURSE NOTES

For my beautiful son Oliver

Orders: please contact Bookpoint Ltd, 130 Milton Park, Abingdon, Oxon OX14 4SB. Telephone: (44) 01235 827720. Fax: (44) 01235 400454. Lines are open from 9.00 - 5.00, Monday to Saturday, with a 24 hour message answering service. You can also order through our website **www.hoddereducation.co.uk**

If you have any comments to make about this, or any of our other titles, please send them to educationenquiries@hodder.co.uk

British Library Cataloguing in Publication Data
A catalogue record for this title is available from the British Library

ISBN: 978 1 444 16308 7

First Edition Published 2012

Impression number	10 9 8 7 6 5 4 3 2 1
Year	2015 2014 2013 2012

Hachette UK's policy is to use papers that are natural, renewable and recyclable products and made from wood grown in sustainable forests. The logging and manufacturing processes are expected to conform to the environmental regulations of the country of origin.

Cover photo © peng wu / iStockphoto
Typeset by Datapage (India) Pvt. Ltd.
Printed and bound in Spain for Hodder Education, An Hachette UK Company, 338 Euston Road, London NW1 3BH

Contents

Guide to the book

Check new words and essential legal terms and what they mean

Definition

Invitation to treat: To invite an offer. An expression of willingness to negotiate.

Test your legal knowledge! Practice makes perfect – answer questions on what you've just read

Workpoint

What reasons did the court give for dismissing the action brought in *Kleinwort Benson Ltd v Malaysia Mining Corporation Bhd* (1989)?

Questions to help you delve deeper into the law and to guide your further reading

Research Point

Is it the case that when assessing merchandise standards considerations of safety are taken into account? Consider *Shine v General Guarantee Corporation* (1988).

Provides examples and extracts from the key cases and judgements you need to know

Case:	
***Roscorla v Thomas* (1842)**	The seller of a horse stated that the horse was, 'sound and free from vice'. Although the opposite was true, because the promise was made **after** the sale of the horse there was no action for misrepresentation.

Diagrams illustrate key points for visual learners

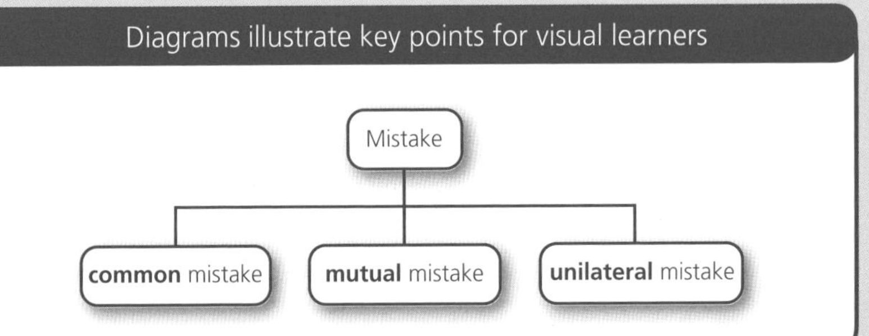

Tick off what you have learnt and check you're on track

Checkpoint - discharge of contracts

I can state the different ways a contract may be discharged	
I can explain the strict rule and exceptions to the strict rule where a contract is discharged by performance	

Provide you with potential real-life exam questions. Answers are available on the accompanying website.

Potential exam questions:

1) Bizhan wrote to Odele on Saturday offering 20 pairs of designer shoes at £30 per pair. Odele wrote back declaring that she was very much interested but asking two questions:

a) Was there any extra charge for postage and packaging?

b) Were the shoes genuine designer shoes?

On Monday whilst on her lunch break Odele went into town to do some shopping. Realising just how expensive designer shoes were now in the shops, Odele emailed Bizhan when she got back to the office. The email stated, 'Accept your price of £30 per pair of shoes'.

Assuming the shoes are genuine designer shoes, is there a contract? If yes, is delivery included in the price?

Guide to the website

There is useful additional material online to support your learning of criminal law. Login at www.hodderplus.co.uk/law

Interactive questions to help you revise aspects of the law

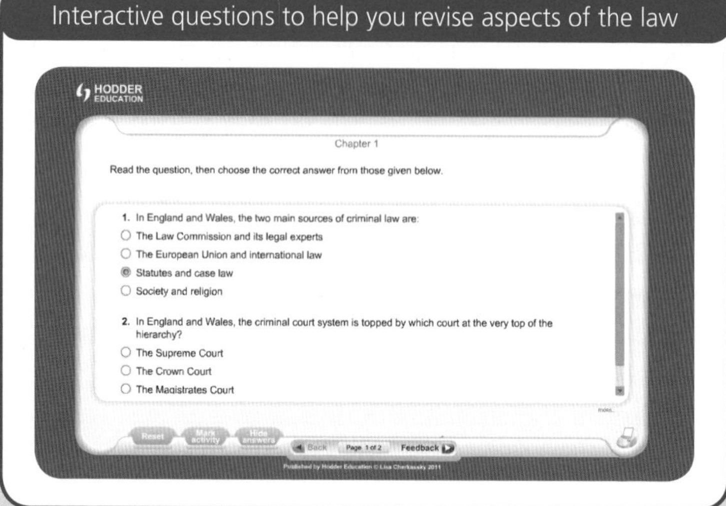

Model Answers

Chapter 1

1. When the criminal law prosecutes and sentences criminals, its purpose is to:

   - incapacitate the criminal
   - punish the criminal
   - deter the criminal and the public
   - reform the criminal
   - educate the criminal and the public
   - affirm moral standards and restore justice in society.

Useful links to websites to help you research further your studies in law

www.parliament.uk
The official Parliament website; use it to track all criminal bills currently before Parliament, explore the role of the House of Lords in law-making, and search for delegated legislation.

www.legislation.gov.uk
The official website for the Stationary Office; use it to search for newly enacted and revised legislation, draft legislation and statutory instruments for the United Kingdom, Scotland, Northern Ireland and Wales.

Acknowledgements

Firstly I would like to give express thanks to those that have worked and provided assistance in the book's production, especially Lucy Winder, Jasmin Naim and Mathew Sullivan. Your continued support and patience has been very much a virtue.

I would like to pay tribute to Natalie, my loving partner and devoted mother to our son Oliver, who deserves unreserved gratitude and appreciation for the support she has given me whilst I have endeavoured to finish this book.

Also, I would like to thank my aviator brother Adam for all the love and guidance that has provided much appreciated career encouragement. A tribute should also be paid to my father whose work ethic is a true inspiration to anyone privileged enough to meet him.

I would like to give a mention for the support and assistance given by Anthony Smith, thank you 'Fonzy'.

And of course the blessing of Oliver Beau and Emily Jane, I revel in your smiles, happiness and the joy that you bring to our family. I hope this book is a source of pride in years to come.

Daniel Rahnavard
August 2012

Preface

The Course Notes series is intended to provide students with useful notes, which are presented in a way that helps with visual learning.

The series is also interactive with:

- Workpoints for students to work through
- Research Points where students are invited to further their knowledge and understanding by referring to important source materials
- Checkpoints to see whether the reader has understood/ learned the key points on each topic
- Examination style questions at the end of each chapter.

There is also support available on the companion website where students can check their own answers to the examination-style questions against the suggested answers on the site, as well as interactive questions and useful links for research.

Jacqueline Martin

Course Notes: Contract Law

Contract law is one of the foundations of studying law. We make contracts all the time, often without realising it and sometimes with everything at stake. For example a contract was agreed when you bought your season ticket, when you bought your car from a dealership and every time your online business takes delivery from a supplier.

The aim of this book is to provide the reader with the key principles of contract law supported by statutes, cases and judicial precedent. The book also lends itself as an extremely useful revision aid for exams. Terms are explained, points illustrated and you are engaged with research and working tasks throughout.

Whether studying contract law in business or law, vocationally or academically, in further or higher education, this book will provide an easily digestible companion. A student-centred approach encourages autonomy and signposts further reading of cases, statutes and legal doctrine.

It is suggested that this book is best served as a compliment to the main texts on contract law. In the same way that butter compliments bread or chips compliment fish one is inherently enhanced by the other. The book has been kept deliberately succinct to allow students to quickly grasp key principles, check understanding, support revision and prepare for the moment the page is turned over on the contract law exam paper.

Daniel Rahnavard

Table of Cases

Table of Statutes

Chapter 1

The origins of contract law, definition and evolution

Definition

Contract: 'A contract is an agreement giving rise to obligations which are enforced or recognised by law. The factor which distinguishes contractual from other legal obligations is that they are based on the agreement of the contracting parties.'

Sir Guenter Treitel *The Law of Contract* (13th edition, Sweet & Maxwell, 2010)

- Put simply a contract is a promise enforceable by law.
- The promise may be one in which a party agrees to do or not to do something.
- Should one party fail to keep their 'promise' the other party is entitled to legal remedy.
- Ordinarily a contract is formed by the mutual assent of two (or more) parties.
- One party makes an offer and the other accepts.

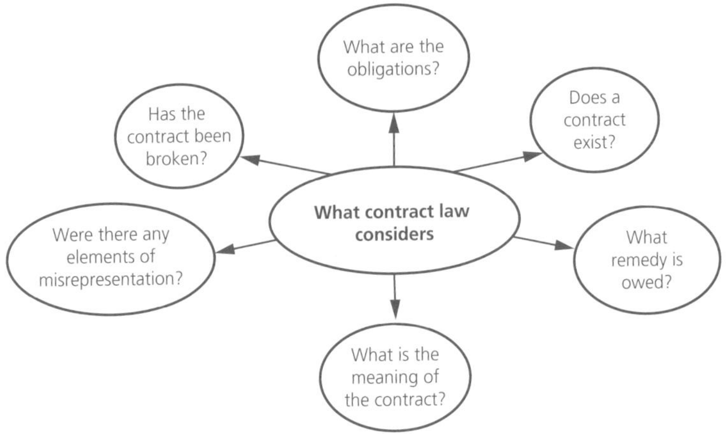

- Contracts are negotiated and agreed every day in the world of business.
- In the commercial world a commercial bargain (or contract) involves goods and/or services being offered for a price.
- A contract may be written or verbal but in order to be legally binding it must contain:
  1. a valid offer
  2. an unqualified acceptance
  3. an intention to create legal relations
  4. valuable consideration
  5. genuine consent (i.e. in the absence of fraud or duress).
- English contract law is principally a case law subject and there is no contract law 'code'.
- The most prominent statutes in contract law are:
  - The Limitation Act 1980
  - Misrepresentation Act 1967
  - Sale of Goods Act 1979
  - Law of Property Act 1925
  - Unfair Contract Terms Act 1977
  - Law Reform (Frustrated Contracts) Act 1943
  - Supply of Goods and Services Act 1982
  - Contracts (Rights of Third Parties) Act 1999
  - Unfair Terms in Consumer Contracts Regulations 1999

Research Point

1) What is the limitation period in which a party may bring an action for breach of a contract under the Limitation Act 1980 and how does this differ in respect of deeds?

2) Which section of the Law of Property Act 1925 concerns the limitation period for deposits?

Workpoint

Write down five different contracts that you have recently made.

1.1 Evolution

1.1.1 12th century

Contract law can trace its history as far back as the 12th century. It stemmed from new interest in land, the ownership of land and rights in property.

- Two types of contract in respect of rights were enforced through the 12th century.

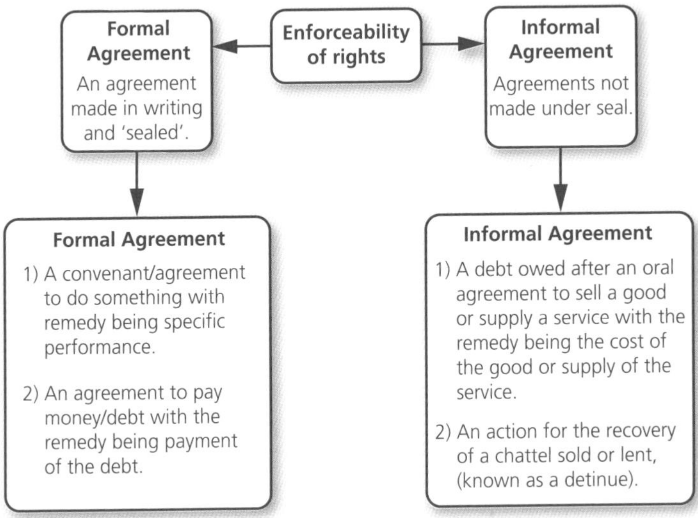

Definition

Detinue: An action for deliverance of a chattel.

Assumpsit: A common law form of action allowing a party relief for a breach of contract or a breach of an informal promise.

1.1.2 13th and 14th centuries

- The law of assumpsit can be traced to the 14th century.
- The assumpsit was a promise by one person undertaking an obligation to another in writing or orally but nevertheless not under seal. An action of covenant would be used instead if the agreement was made under seal.
- If the defendant failed to perform the undertaking or carry out a promise it gave rise to assumpsit as a cause of action.

- The Judicature Acts of 1873 and 1875 abolished the assumpsit cause of action.

1.1.3 16th and 17th centuries

- The doctrine of consideration was created around this time.
- It is not quite clear how or why this doctrine came about but what is clear is that the unlimited and imprecise nature of assumpsit needed to be managed.
- In order for a promise to be given legal effect there had to be a reason (or motive) for it.
- Consideration and the notion of contracts being built on the exchange of promises is what underpins contract law in its modern format.
- The definition given by Sir Frederick Pollock, approved by Lord Dunedin in *Dunlop v Selfridge Ltd* (1915), is as follows:

'An act or forebearance of one party, or the promise thereof, is the price for which the promise of the other is bought, and the promise thus given for value is enforceable.'

Definition

Consideration: The price paid by one party for the other party's promise.

1.1.4 19th century and the freedom of contract

- The rules of contract law were largely formulated in the 19th century.
- Britain was building upon the industrial revolution, *laissez-faire* economics and the concept of a free market. This was a time when a person was more the master of his own destiny, and there was the idea that rather than the government it should be market forces and economic principles that presided over people's relationships with one another.
- Freedom of contract is exactly that. A party is free to negotiate, including such terms they see fit and agreeing on a wide range of matters.
- The freedom of contract principle encompasses the following rules and liberties:

• Parties are free to enter into negotiations which are intended to be legally binding. →	• This can be explicit or otherwise. The courts will also protect those parties who made an agreement but never had any intention to be legally bound.
• Elements of misrepresentation are examples of freedom of contract. →	• The court will set aside any agreement where a party was not in possession of all the facts, was coerced, mistaken or assented based on false information.
• The courts are concerned with the actual existence of a contract. →	• The court takes no interest where a party is a victim of a bad bargain where the bargain was freely entered into.
• The freedom to include terms and conditions that the parties so wish. →	• Terms which are clearly disadvantageous to one party will still be permitted by the court where the parties had equal bargaining power and freely accepted the terms that they assented to.
• There has to be a valid offer and a valid acceptance to constitute an agreement or *consensus ad idem* between the parties. →	• For example the Unsolicited Goods and Services Act 1971 prevents a party from receiving payment for goods that were never requested or accepted.

Research Point

Which of the above rules/liberties concerning freedom of contract is supported by *Williams v Roffey Bros & Nicholls Contractors Ltd* (1990)?

Definition

Consensus ad idem: The agreement made between the parties.

1.1.5 20th century consumer and social protectionism

- The landscape of Britain changed in the 19th and 20th centuries. The notion of freedom of contract was not as prevalent. There were many reasons for this including politics, economics, spending power and the very nature of day to day society.

- Industry grew bigger and so did consumerism because of Britain's position on the global stage as an industrial powerhouse.
- Following this, individuals began to lose their negotiating equality with large companies. The relationship changed with large companies using standard form contracts, increasing their financial influence and widening the gap between them and the ordinary man by creating products that required particular expertise.
- A movement towards protectionism arose from this disparity in bargaining power.
- Legislation was introduced by Parliament to encourage greater equality; this was later followed by protection from the European Union.
- Whilst contracts made between businesses were protected to an extent, the individual was protected more. Parliament particularly imposed conditions on sellers of goods and sought to protect consumers who could now expect certain basic standards.
- For private individuals contracting with businesses, there was still freedom of contract but with the buyer buying at his own risk. A view summed up by the phrase *caveat emptor*.

Definition

Caveat emptor: Let the buyer beware.

1.1.6 The present day – a change of policy

- As can be seen above, Parliament and the courts made strenuous efforts to protect freedom of contract whilst preventing attempts towards economic monopoly or oligopoly.
- Margaret Thatcher's government sought to resurrect freedom of contract in the 1980s. This was done through privatisation of publicly owned and state controlled utilities.
- The government believed that the social and consumer protectionist policies brought in by previous governments were stifling Britain's economic potential.
- The effect of privatisation was financial accountability. Previously state owned companies that wanted to make a profit were now answerable to:
  - consumers
  - shareholders
  - watchdogs

- the media
- regulators.

- This benefitted the individual. Rather than depending on the state for a pension, for example, individuals had the freedom to choose and organise their own pensions. By reducing protectionism and promoting freedom of contract the government felt the individual was more 'in the know' and educated and thus better able to protect their own interests.

Workpoint

Produce a timeline showing the evolution and development of contract law from the 12th century through to the present day.

1.2 Contract law, criminal law and tort law

- The relationship between contract law and the law of tort is often seen to be close. The reality is that it is often too close and the overlaps are complicated.

Similarities	Differences
• Victims can claim damages for harm done to them.	• In contract parties impose obligations themselves and only fulfil those obligations to the extent agreed before the contract was formalised. • In tort duties apply to everyone and are imposed by law.
• Duties and obligations are owed by one party to another in both contract and tort law.	• In contract law the duty and obligations are owed only to the other party. • In tort there is a duty owed to anyone who is likely to be affected.
• Both are subject to the Limitation Act 1980 and have limitations of 6 years. However in contract the limitation period is 12 years where the contract is created by deed. Also in negligence personal injury matters have a 3 year limitation period.	• 'in cases of breach of contract the cause of action arises at the date of the breach of contract'; but 'in tort the cause of action arises, not when the culpable conduct occurs, but when the plaintiff first sustains damage'. *Nykredit Mortgage Bank plc v Edward Erdman Group (No. 2)* (1997)

- Often the relationship may involve both a common law or extra contractual duty to exercise reasonable care, and an implied statutory condition, at the same time. The overlapping rights and duties in contract and tort pose the question, 'does one sue a contractor in contract law or a manufacturer in tort?'
- A claimant may pick a cause of action or indeed run a 'concurrence' of claims where the tort of negligence imposed duty of care overlaps the contractual duty of care (see the House of Lords in *Henderson v Merrett Syndicates Ltd* (1995)).
- The criminal law involves itself particularly in matters of contracts that concern consumer protection. Whilst freedom of contract has not gone away neither has protectionism. Trading Standards Departments are empowered to bring prosecutions and are proactive in their protection of the individual consumer.
- Criminal law statutes can be used to protect the consumer and control contracts. They include:
  - Consumer Protection Act 1987
  - Food Safety Act 1990
  - Trade Descriptions Act 1968
  - Consumer Credit Act 1974
  - Consumer Protection (Distance Selling) Regulations 2000
  - Package Travel, Package Holidays and Package Tours Regulations 1992

1.3 The objective principle

- At the heart of contract law is the objective principle and it is fundamental to acceptance.

Definition

> The objective principle: 'A person's words or conduct must be interpreted in the manner in which another might objectively and reasonably understand them.'
>
> Lord Steyn, 'Contract Law: Fulfilling the Reasonable Expectations of Honest Men' (1997) 113 LQR 433

- In *McCutcheon v David MacBrayne Ltd* (1964) Lord Reid said:

  'the judicial task is not to discover the actual intentions of each party; it is to decide what each was reasonably entitled to conclude from the attitude of the other'.

- The objective principle could be said to concern itself with the following:
  - Is there a contract? If yes, on what terms?
  - Has a voidable contract been 'affirmed' by a party?
  - Has a party rejected the agreement? If yes, has the other party accepted the rejection?
  - Has the contract been varied or ended by agreement?

Workpoint

How is contract law similar to tort law? What are the main differences?

Research Point

Since the UK first became a member of the European Union on 1st January 1973 (specifically the European Economic Community (EEC)), how have treaty articles, directives and regulations affected English contract law?

Checkpoint – origins of contract law, definition and evolution

Item on checklist:	Done!
I can give a clear definition of a contract	
I can explain the requirements of a legally binding contract	
I can define the main statutes affecting the area of contract law	
I can differentiate between formal and informal agreements	
I can explain the law of assumpsit and what Act of Parliament abolished it	
I can define the freedom of contract principle and at what point in history it originated	
I can explain the relationship between contract law and tort law	

Chapter 2
Creating a contract

2.1 Formation of contracts

A contract can be described as a legally enforceable agreement between two (or more) parties. The parties negotiate and should the negotiations be long and protracted it may be difficult to determine whether agreement has been reached. It should also not be assumed that further negotiations will automatically bring the agreement to an end.

When deciding upon whether an agreement is a legally binding contract the courts apply the fundamental components of a legally binding contract (see below) and decide whether the same terms have been agreed (see *Kennedy v Lee* (1817)).

Contracts are a part of everyday life. As such it is imperative that parties understand not only their rights and responsibilities in respect of the contract but also the terms contained therein.

A contract is formed when the following exist:

- the intention to create legal relations
- consideration
- an offer by one party (A)
- acceptance of the offer by another party (B).

Case:	
***Crest Nicholson (Londinium) Ltd v Akaria Investments Ltd* (2010)**	The question was whether a letter received by Akaria Investments Ltd from Crest Nicholson contained an offer that was capable of acceptance, therefore enabling the formation of a contract which in turn would determine the correct basis for profit payment calculation.

- A contract is a legally binding agreement.
- There can be several parties to a contract and contracts may be formed by organisations, groups or individuals.

- When each party carries out their side of the bargain, thus honouring an agreement, a contract is completed.
- The making of an offer is the first fundamental component in the process of forming a legal contract: an offer, an acceptance of the offer, the intention to create legal relations and an exchange of consideration.
- There are rules which, if satisfied, show that a contract has been formed and exists.
- No matter how many parties are involved and despite the complexities of any arrangements the same rules will apply.

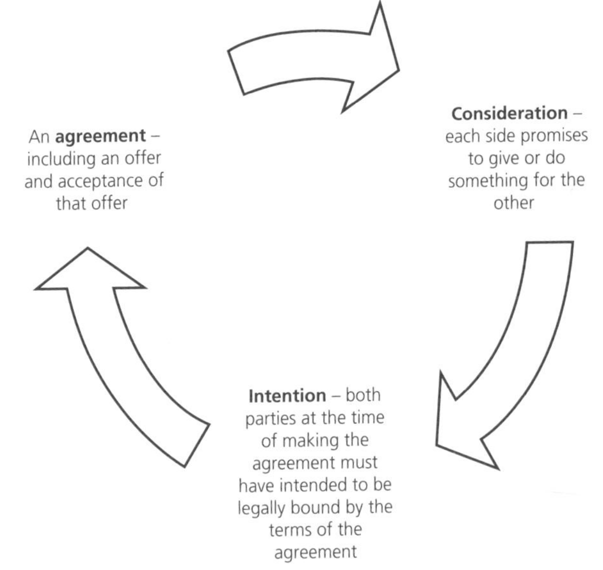

Bilateral contract	An exchange of promises between two parties. Neither party may have done anything to implement an agreement; however once promises are exchanged the contract is valid. **Example** – Oliver telephones Emily and promises to pay her £5,000 for her car. Emily telephones Oliver back, accepts the offer and promises to give Oliver her car for £5,000.
Unilateral contract	A party makes an offer; it is accepted by the offeree through the performance of his/her side of the bargain. Only one party makes a promise so the contract is unilateral.

Example – Adam has lost his cat Smudge and puts up a reward poster offering £50 to anyone who finds the cat. Karen finds Smudge and returns it to Adam. Karen (the offeree) has acted on the promise of Adam (the offeror) and as such Adam is legally obliged to fulfil the contract. Karen, as the offeree, could not be forced to act (find the cat) because the offeror had not received a return promise. Adam's is the only enforceable promise that exists once Karen has found the cat.

2.2 Offer

An offer is an expression of willingness by the offeror to contract on a set of specific terms and/or conditions with the intention to be bound by the contract once the offer is accepted. The existence of an offer, either verbally or in writing, must be proved.

Note that in law a legitimate offer will not exist if external obligations, outside of the terms and conditions of the offer, are placed on the offeree. The problem here is the offeree may be prejudiced from reaching an agreement and accepting the offer.

Definition

Offeror: The person, group, organisation making the offer.

Offeree: The person, group, organisation receiving the offer.

- The offer must be made with the intention that it should be legally binding.
- The terms of the offer must be definite, clear and unambiguous. Both parties, if accepting of the terms, must know what they have agreed to.
- An offer must be communicated to the offeree. The offeree cannot accept something they do not know of.
- The offer may be made by any method be it verbally, in writing or by conduct.
- In the offer, the offeror will have clearly stipulated the terms which, should the offer be accepted, he or she will be bound by. Remember, should the offeree not accept these terms, there will be no contract. There must be acceptance.

- The offeree must be free to accept the terms of a contract without undue influence or extra obligations being imposed which are not terms of the contract. The offer would not be legal.
- An offer can be in any format including **express** or **implied**.
- An express offer could be made in writing or orally. For example Chloe writes to Nick offering to buy his car for £1,000.
- An implied offer from conduct could occur, for example when filling a car with petrol at the petrol station.
- An offer can be made to specific parties or individuals or in general and not limited to any party in particular.

Research Point

***Carlill v Carbolic Smoke Ball Co.* (1893)**

- What were the facts of the case?
- What type of contract did the case concern?
- What were the defence arguments put forward?
- Why did the Court of Appeal reject the defence according to Bowen LJ?

Case:	
***O'Brien v MGN Ltd* (2001)**	Facts: The claimant purchased a Sunday newspaper containing a 'scratchcard'. The claimant's card had £50,000 revealed in two 'windows'. The *Daily Mirror* was holding a competition the following week in which the scratchcard could be used. The claimant believed he had won £50,000 when, the following week, he bought a *Daily Mirror* newspaper and in accordance with the rules rang the hotline where he was told the prize for the day was £50,000. Held: The advertisement in the *Daily Mirror* was considered by the court to be an offer and when those with a winning scratchcard called to claim their prize the offer was accepted. See also *Bowerman v ABTA* (1996).

Workpoint

Natalie, who is 26, goes to a fancy dress shop and says to the manager, 'I will sell you my nurses' uniform for £35.'

1) Has a clear offer been made?
2) What are the reasons for your answer?

The formation of a contract explained thus far is relatively straightforward. However this is not always the case and whilst it may be perceived that in some way an offer is being made, the reality can often be something different. That is generally categorised as an invitation to treat.

Workpoint

Define the terms offer and acceptance. Explain the rules regarding offer.

Checkpoint – contract formation

Item on checklist:	Done!
I can give a description of a contract	
I can describe and explain the four components of a contract	
I can define a unilateral contract	
I can define a bilateral contract	
I can explain why acceptance is important to the formation of contract	
I can give case examples of a contract	
I can define an offeror	
I can define an offeree	
I understand how a contract is formed	
I can define an express offer	
I can define an implied offer	

2.3 Offers and invitations to treat – how to distinguish

Definition

Invitation to treat: To invite an offer. An expression of willingness to negotiate.

An invitation to treat can often appear to be a contractual offer. Distinguishing between an offer and an invitation to treat is extremely important.

- An invitation to treat is not recognised in law as an offer.
- An invitation to treat is where one party is inviting another to make an offer. Having considered the offer the original party can then choose to reject or accept the offer. In the case of an offer all that is required is the acceptance of the original party.
- If a party merely wishes to commence negotiations and not be bound by the terms of an offer then this is an invitation to treat. The other party is invited to make an offer.
- The court will not necessarily consider the wording of a statement when considering if there was an offer or an invitation to treat. It would be more mindful of the intention of parties and the surrounding circumstances.

Offer	Invitation to treat
Where an offer is made and accepted a legally binding contractual agreement is made.	A party may simply wish to invite offers or expressions of interest (an invitation to treat).
For example, if Karen says to Tony 'would you like to buy my wheelbarrow for £30?', then Tony would only need to say, 'Yes, I would like to buy your wheelbarrow for £30'. Here there is clearly recognisable **offer** and **acceptance** (the essential ingredients for a contract).	For example, Karen puts her wheelbarrow in her shop window with a £30 price tag on it. Tony, having seen the wheelbarrow and price in the window walks into the shop and makes an offer of £30 for the wheelbarrow. This is a clear example of an invitation to treat by Karen. She has invited another party to make an offer. If she accepts an offer only then is a contract formed. Remember – Karen having issued the advertisement has the prerogative to reject any offers to buy the wheelbarrow at £30.

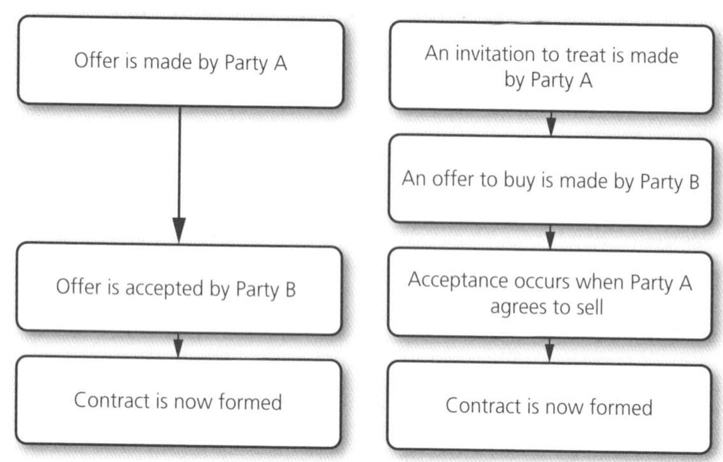

The stages of contract formation where there is an invitation to treat and a traditional offer and acceptance are shown above.

Three classic situations in which there is an invitation to treat but not an offer are:

- auction sales
- goods on display in shop windows or on shelves in self service stores
- advertisements with goods listed for sale on the Internet or in magazines, catalogues and newspapers.

1. *Auction sales* – putting something into an auction or 'up' for auction does not constitute an offer. It is deemed an invitation to treat.

Case:	
***British Car Auctions v Wright* (1972)**	Any bids amount to offers thus enabling the auctioneer to either accept or reject them.

Auctions are usually with or without a reserve. Without a reserve means the auctioneer, regardless of how low the bid is, will sell to whoever bids the highest.

Case:	
***Warlow v Harrison* (1859)**	It was held that requesting bids constituted an offer to accept the highest bid and by bidding the offer must be accepted.

Should the auctioneer refuse to sell (to the highest bidder) he or she may be sued for breach of contract.

Case:	
***Barry v Heathcote Ball & Co. (Commercial Auctions) Ltd* (2000)**	Two lots of machinery worth £14,251 advertised as 'without reserve' were withdrawn by an auctioneer from auction. The claimant had made bids of £200 for each lot, which were the highest bids. These were refused by the auctioneer and he subsequently sold them for £750 privately. The claimant sued and argued that the auctioneer was legally obliged to accept his bid as he was the highest bidder since an auctioneer was offering to accept the highest bid in auctions held without reserve.

If there is a reserve price, no sale and no contract will be formed if bidding fails to reach the reserve price. See *McManus v Fortescue* (1907).

2. *Goods on display in shop windows or on shelves in self service stores*

Case:	
***Fisher v Bell* (1961)**	Facts: A prosecution for 'offering for sale' prohibited weapons under the now repealed Restriction of Offensive Weapons Act 1961 was brought. Held: The court decided that there was an invitation to treat and not an offer where the shopkeeper had displayed a flick knife with a price tag in his shop window.

Research Point

***Pharmaceutical Society of Great Britain v Boots Cash Chemists (Southern) Ltd* (1952)**

What were the facts of the case?

What important legal principle was established in this case?

Why was this case more problematic than *Fisher v Bell* (1961)?

3. *Goods listed for sale on the Internet or in magazines, catalogues and newspapers*

   The advertisement is only an invitation to treat. The party making the advertisement has to accept an offer made by the party reading it in order for a contract to be formed.

Case:	
***Partridge v Crittenden* (1968)**	The defendant was prosecuted unsuccessfully for offering for sale a wild bird under the Protection of Birds Act 1954. He had placed an advertisement stating 'Bramblefinch cocks, bramblefinch hens, 25s each'. The court held this was an invitation to treat and not an offer.

The same principle applies to price lists, circulars, timetables and catalogues as it does to small advertisements in newspapers, magazines or on the Internet.

Just because a party suggests a price which they deem to be appropriate does not make it an offer.

Case:	
***Harvey v Facey* (1893)**	Facey received a telegraph from Harvey asking, 'Will you sell me Bumper Hall Pen? Telegraph lowest price'. Facey's telegraph stated, 'Lowest cash price for Bumper Hall Pen £900'. Harvey sent another telegram, 'we agree to buy Bumper Hall Pen for £900 asked by you. Please send us your title deeds in order that we may get early possession'. The action brought by Harvey failed since Facey's reply was merely a declaration of the lowest price required if and when he decides to sell; his reply was not an offer, only a response to a request for information. See also *Gibson v Manchester City Council* (1979).

Case:	
***Grainger v Gough* (1896)**	Lord Herschell commented, 'The transmission of such a price list does not amount to an offer to supply an unlimited quantity of the wine described at the price named, so that as soon as an order is given there is a binding contract to supply that quantity.'

- Invitations to tender for the supply of goods or services are invitations to treat. Party A tendering out services does not have to sign a contract with party B just because they are the first party submitting a tender proposal. They may opt for party C or D if they submit better proposals.
- Remember that the formation of a contract requires acceptance.
- In *Spencer v Harding* (1870) it was decided the party inviting the tenders is free to accept any of them and not necessarily the cheapest or in fact any of them at all.

Matters not tantamount to an invitation to treat:

- In certain circumstances or owing to the words used what appears to be a *prima facie* invitation to treat is in fact an offer. The choice of words is of significance. Examples include:

Circumstance:	Case:
Advertisements involving a unilateral offer	*Carlill v Carbolic Smoke Ball Co. Ltd* (1893)
A statement of price where an offer is also intended	*Biggs v Boyd Gibbins* (1971)
Competitive tendering	*Harvela Investments Ltd v Royal Trust Co. of Canada Ltd* (1986)

Definition

Prima facie: On first appearance.

Checkpoint – offer and invitation to treat

Item on checklist:	**Done!**
I can define what makes an offer	
I can define what makes an invitation to treat	
I can state the differences between an offer and an invitation to treat	
I can give examples of invitations to treat	
I can list situations which are considered invitations to treat rather than offers	
I can give case examples of invitations to treat	
I can list the rules relating to the communication of an offer	

Workpoint

Make a list of five situations that are considered invitations to treat rather than offers and name one case and its facts for each situation.

2.4 Termination of offers

'Agreement' is one of the fundamentals of a legally binding contract. However should an offer no longer exist or be withdrawn there can be no agreement and an enforceable contract is not in existence.

- An offer can be brought to an end at any point before acceptance and in a number of different ways:

Acceptance or refusal	If the offeree agrees to be bound by the terms of the offer a contract is formed. Acceptance may be in writing, orally or by conduct. Alternatively the offer is refused and there is no contract.
Failure of a precondition	Offers can be made subject to certain conditions. A failure to meet certain conditions will mean the offer is no longer open to acceptance. For example a footballer offers to sell his boots to a fan if he is given new boots when he signs for a new club.
Counter-offer	Any attempt by the offeree to introduce a new term is a counter-offer and not acceptance of the original offer. The counter-offer is an automatic rejection of the original offer: *Hyde v Wrench* (1840).
Lapse of time	An offer, if not subject to a specific time limit, will lapse after a reasonable period. Reasonable depends on the circumstances. An offer to sell perishable goods would lapse after a few days, equally so unpredictable commodities like shares. In *Ramsgate Victoria Hotel Co. Ltd v Montefiore* (1866) an offer to buy shares in June had lapsed by November. A time limit must be complied with if specified.
Death	The effect of death upon an offer is somewhat a grey area and there is currently no legal precedent for dealing with circumstances where the offeree has died. Nevertheless an offer will lapse if the offeree dies and his representatives are unable to accept on his behalf as in *Reynolds v Atherton* (1921). If the offeror dies, *Bradbury v Morgan* (1862) suggests his representatives may still be bound by an acceptance that is made in ignorance of the death of the offeror.

2.4.1 Revocation

Definition

Revocation: Withdrawal of an offer.

- Revocation forms part of the 'freedom of contract' concept.
- Revocation is effected if sent by fax or email within normal business working hours but not read until some time later, or if it is delivered to the last known address.
- An offer may be revoked that was made to the public at large if sufficient steps are taken to notify those to whom it was made. For example if an offer was made on the Town Hall notice board, it would suffice to place the revocation notice in the same place.
- Revocation must occur prior to acceptance (*Routledge v Grant* (1828)).

Workpoint

Is it possible for an offer to be revoked by a third party?

HINT! See *Dickinson v Dodds* (1876).

- The revocation must be communicated. In *Byrne v Van Tienhoven* (1880) it was held that revocation of the offer was invalid because acceptance had occurred prior to revocation.

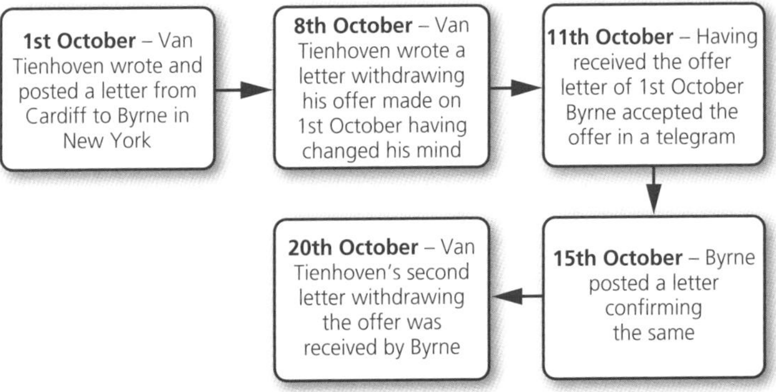

- Where there is a unilateral contract offer this will be treated by the courts as irrevocable once performance has commenced by the offeree.

Research Point

What was the House of Lords decision in *Luxor (Eastbourne) Ltd v Cooper* (1941)?

Do you agree with their decision?

Research Point

In *Errington v Errington & Woods* (1952) Lord Denning explained the principle of law known as the 'Errington Principle'.

What is this principle?

2.5 Acceptance

Definition

Acceptance: The communication of an unequivocal and unconditional agreement to a valid offer.

'final and unqualified expression of assent to the terms of an offer' (*Chitty on Contracts*, Ch. 2-027)

2.5.1 Rules on acceptance

Acceptance is one of the fundamentals of a legally binding contractual agreement. Without valid acceptance of a valid offer there can be no legally binding contract. For proof of a valid acceptance there should be:

- An unequivocal and unconditional acceptance of the offer.
- Effective communication of the acceptance.

Workpoint

Create a timeline of *Hyde v Wrench* (1840) showing the key factual points.

Do you agree with Lord Langdale's reasoning?

- The state of mind of the offeree is the decisive factor when deciding if the offeror is bound by the acceptance. This gives a part subjective, part objective test which needs to be satisfied.

Research Point

Do the cases of *Fitch v Snedaker* (1868) and *R v Clarke* (1927) support or contradict the decision given in *Tinn v Hoffman and Co.* (1873)?

- If terms or conditions are added to the acceptance then a counter-offer is created. The original offer is no longer open to acceptance.
- A debate over ancillary matters amounts to a counter-offer and as such is an outright rejection of the original offer. *Jones v Daniel* (1894) confirms this.
- When considering post-contractual negotiations, correspondence between the parties is scrutinised by the court to pinpoint when and whether an unequivocal acceptance has been made. Should acceptance have taken place, then unless there has been an attempt to rescind the contract, a legally binding contract will be in existence regardless of further negotiations (*Perry v Suffields Ltd* (1916)).

Definition

Counter-offer: The changing of an important term or the suggestion of an alternative set of terms by the offeree.

- Enquiries or requests for further information do not count as a rejection of the offer where the enquiry does not seek to alter the terms or conditions of the offer.

Case:	
***Stevenson, Jaques & Co. v Mclean* (1880)**	The claimant asked whether he could buy goods on credit after the defendant had offered to sell him iron with the offer remaining open until the following Monday. Stephenson telegraphed a full acceptance on the Monday having not received a reply from the defendant. Here, asking to buy the goods on credit was simply a request for information and as such the offer was still open to acceptance.

Workpoint

Match the cases below to the legal principles opposite.

Jones v Daniel (1894)	Requests for information do not count as a rejection of the original offer
Davies & Co v William Old (1969)	Acceptance must be unequivocal
Compagnie de Commerce et Commissions SARL v Parkinson Stove Co. (1953)	Technical counter-offers of no importance to the parties will not count as a rejection of the offer
Pars Technology Ltd v City Link Transport Holdings Ltd (1999)	A disagreement over ancillary rather than central terms will amount to a rejection of the original offer and will be a counter-offer
Stevenson v Mclean (1880)	Acceptance can be in any form as long as it is effective; however if there is a required form then in order for it to be valid the acceptance must be presented in that form
Brogden v Metropolitan Railway Co. (1877)	A counter-offer, if accepted, can become a term of the agreement
Hyde v Wrench (1840)	It is not possible to benefit from both the original offer and the counter-offer

2.5.2 The means of acceptance

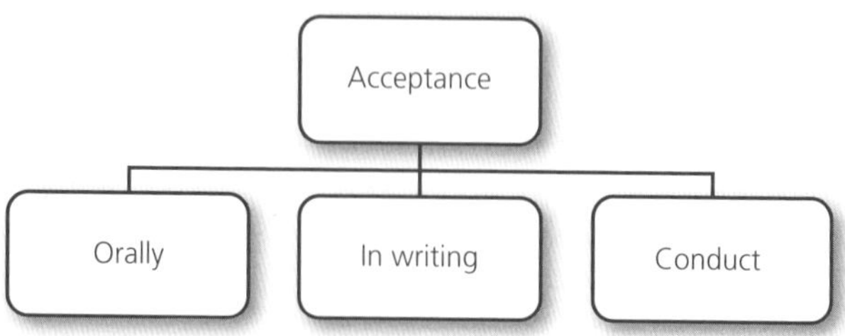

- A valid acceptance can be given orally, in written form or inferred from conduct. A valid acceptance given orally or in writing tends to create little complexity.

- Acceptance of the offer is provided once what is in the offer is put into practice. The court will pay strict attention to the intention and nature of a party's conduct and consider whether or not it is reasonable to infer acceptance was intended.

Case:	
Brogden v Metropolitan Railway Co. (1877)	There had been an agreement in place for some time between the parties for the supply of coal. A more formal arrangement was to be put into place and the railway company sent Brogden a draft contract. A new term was inserted by Brogden and returned to the railway company. This was signed by the railway's company secretary (without being looked at) and filed away. The addition of a new term was considered by the House of Lords to be a counter-offer which was accepted by conduct either when the company allowed delivery or when it next placed an order and paid for the coal.

- Acceptance can occur once the offeree starts using the goods – see *Weatherby v Banham* (1832). This should be considered with caution especially given current legislation, as outlined below.

The Unsolicited Goods and Services Act 1971 protects parties from unprincipled businesses who claim financial recompense for sending unwanted and never requested goods through the post.	**The Consumer Protection (Distance Selling) Regulations 2000 Regulation 24(4)** makes it an offence to request payment for unsolicited goods and/or services.

- *Taylor v Allon* (1966) and *Day Morris Associates v Voyce* (2003) suggest it must be clear that the particular conduct performed by the offeree was done so the absolute intention of accepting the offer.

Research Point

Under which circumstances, as stipulated by the Unsolicited Goods and Services Act 1971, may an individual treat unsolicited goods sent by an offeror as a gift as their own?

Research Point

What were the facts of the case in *Gibbons v Proctor* (1891) and *Williams v Carwardine* (1833)? What were the legal principles? Do you agree with the legal principles?

2.5.3 Communication of acceptance

As with an offer, acceptance must be communicated. It should be communicated by the offeree or a party duly authorised to the offeror.

Case:	
***Holwell Securities Ltd v Hughes* (1974)**	Russell LJ '… It is the law in the first place that, *prima facie*, acceptance of an offer must be communicated to the offeror'.

- Acceptance will not be effective if it is communicated by a party who did not have the required authority to do so.

Case:	
***Powell v Lee* (1908)**	The defendant decided to appoint Powell as a headmaster. Powell found out through a member of the interview panel who was not authorised to disclose the panel's decision. The panel changed its mind and appointed another candidate. Powell sued claiming his offer of services had been accepted. There was no contract since Powell never received official notification that his offer of work had been accepted by the defendant.

Case:	Incorporates two important principles:
***Entores v Miles Far East Corporation* (1955)**	1) Acceptance has not only to be communicated but also received by the offeror. 2) A contract exists where, but for the actions of the offeror, acceptance would have been received.

2.5.4 Silence

Case:	
***Felthouse v Bindley* (1863)**	Silence on its own does not amount to acceptance.
***Nissan UK Ltd v Nissan Motor Manufacturing (UK) Ltd* (1994)**	In the event that a party's actions or conduct appear to suggest an acceptance the general rule that silence does not amount to acceptance can, in consideration of other facts, be negated.

- The offer of a unilateral contract, as in *Carlill v The Carbolic Smoke Ball Co. Ltd* (1893), does not require acceptance or the communication thereof. The Carbolic Smoke Ball Co. in its defence argued that, since there was no communication of acceptance, there was no contract. However, the court stated that unilateral contracts do not require formal acceptance where there was performance in accordance with the terms of the offer.
- *Treitel* (12th edition, London, 2007) confirms in Chapter 2-043 that where there have been previous repeated dealings between the parties silence can amount to acceptance.

Workpoint

Andres and Lionel have long spoken about Andres's antique collection of football memorabilia. Andres has a Barcelona football shirt from the 2011 European Cup final win over Manchester United. Lionel has said on many occasions that, should Andres consider selling his collection or specifically the Barcelona shirt, he would be interested in buying it. Andres, having lost his job, is desperate to raise some money and, having seen a similar a shirt from the same cup final sold in an online auction for £550, leaves Lionel a voicemail on his mobile phone. The voicemail stated, 'Hey Lionel, remember the Barcelona shirt of mine you always wanted? Well it's yours for £550. If I don't hear back from you I'll assume you still want to buy it and you're happy with the price.' Andres never hears from Lionel.

Andres seeks your advice as to whether or not there is a legally binding contract to sell the shirt for £550 to Lionel.

Workpoint

What are the main exceptions to the general requirement that before a contract can arise the offeror should receive notification of acceptance?

2.5.5 Acceptance communicated by post, the 'postal rule'

'The postal rule' →	Acceptance takes place the moment it is validly posted. The rule that acceptance must be communicated is annulled.

- A contract is formed when a letter of acceptance is posted and **not** when acceptance is received. It is therefore at the point of postage that a legally binding contract exists.

Case:	
***Adams v Lindsell* (1818)**	Facts: The defendant posted a letter on 2 September offering to sell some wool, requesting that the claimant accept by post. The defendant had addressed the letter incorrectly and the claimant did not receive it until 5 September. The claimant sent his letter of acceptance that evening. By 7 September the defendant had not received the claimant's acceptance and so he sold the wool the next day to a third party. He then received the claimant's acceptance on 9 September. Held: The Court of Appeal held that there was a contract between the claimant and the defendant. The defendant could not argue the claimant's acceptance had occurred too late and the defendant only had himself to blame that the offer did not get to the defendant sooner.

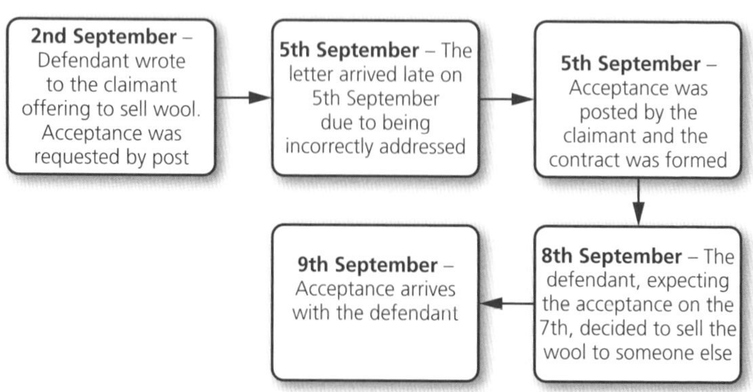

- The 'postal rule' will still be invoked where the letter is lost in the post but was nevertheless properly stamped, addressed and the loss of the letter is not the direct fault of the offeree.

- The postal rule is easily bypassed by the insistence of the offeror that there is no contract until he or she has actually received acceptance.

Case:	Facts:
***Re London and Northern Bank, ex parte Jones* (1900)**	In order for the postal rule to apply, the letter of acceptance must be properly addressed and stamped.
***Household Fire Insurance v Grant* (1879)**	The offeror can prescribe the method of acceptance.
***Holwell Securities v Hughes* (1974)**	Under the terms of Hughes' offer, 'notice in writing' was required for acceptance. When the firm posted its acceptance and the acceptance was never received, the firm argued the postal rule was effective. The court disagreed stating the postal rule could not be applied successfully, given that actual communication of acceptance was required.
***Manchester Diocesan Council for Education v Commercial and General Investments Ltd* (1969)**	J Buckley '… an offeror, who by the terms of his offer insists on acceptance in a particular way, is entitled to insist that he is not bound unless acceptance is effected or communicated in that precise way …'.

- Once acceptance has been correctly posted the offeror can no longer revoke the offer (*Byrne v Van Tienhoven* (1880)).
- *Brinkibon Ltd v Stahag Stahl und Stahlwarenhandelsgellschaft GmbH* (1983) affirmed unequivocally that the Post Office has to be in control of the acceptance for it to be effective. This does not include a postman delivering letters but would include placing the acceptance in a post box or giving it to someone authorised to receive or collect letters on behalf of the Post Office.
- The use of the telephone and more recent communication methods has rendered the postal rule largely obsolete. As long as acceptance is communicated, it is immediate. The same principle applies to email.

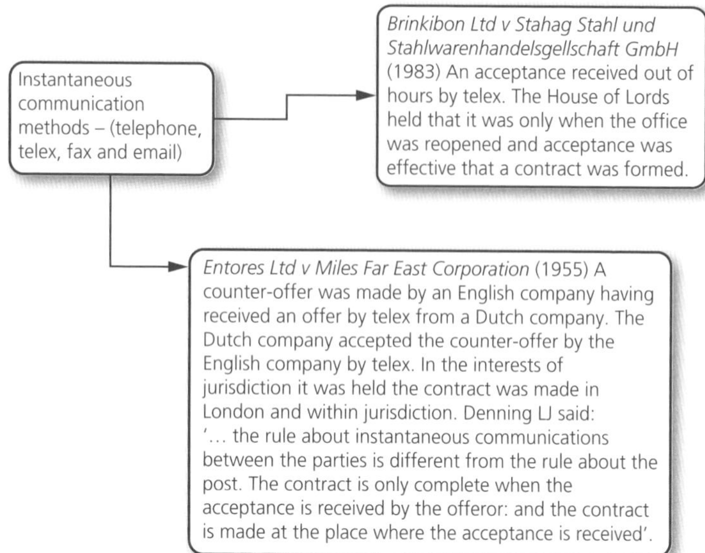

Workpoint

Chloe receives an email from Lucy offering to sell her a greenhouse. Lucy writes in the email that, by 5:30pm tomorrow, Chloe must have informed Lucy of her acceptance otherwise she will offer the greenhouse through an online auction site. Chloe is on holiday and does not check her emails until she gets back, two days after the email had been sent by Lucy. Nevertheless, desperately keen to buy the greenhouse she emails Lucy stating, 'So sorry about the late reply Lucy, I've been absorbing the sun! I would love to buy the greenhouse.'

Advise Chloe on whether she is entitled to the greenhouse.

- Electronic acceptance is governed by:

  1. Electronic Commerce Directive 2000/31
  2. Electronic Commerce (EC Directive) Regulations 2002
  3. Consumer Protection (Distance Selling) Regulations 2000

- No contract is formed electronically until acceptance is received by the buyer as per EU Electronic Commerce Directive 2000/31 and the Electronic Commerce (EC Directive) Regulations 2002

- Article 11 of the Electronic Commerce Directive states:

  'the contract is concluded when the recipient of the service has received from the service provider, electronically, an acknowledgement of receipt of the recipient's acceptance'.

Research Point

What legal rights does a buyer have under the Consumer Protection (Distance Selling) Regulations 2000 in respect of the following:

1) The right to cancel?
2) Description?
3) Price?
4) Arrangement for payment?
5) Seller identity?

2.5.6 'Battle of the forms' – the standard form of contract

- A standard form is a common way for a business to contract with a large amount of potential offerees without the administrative nightmare of negotiating with each individual offeree.
- There isn't often a problem in a consumer sale; however a quandary can arise between the standard forms of different businesses.

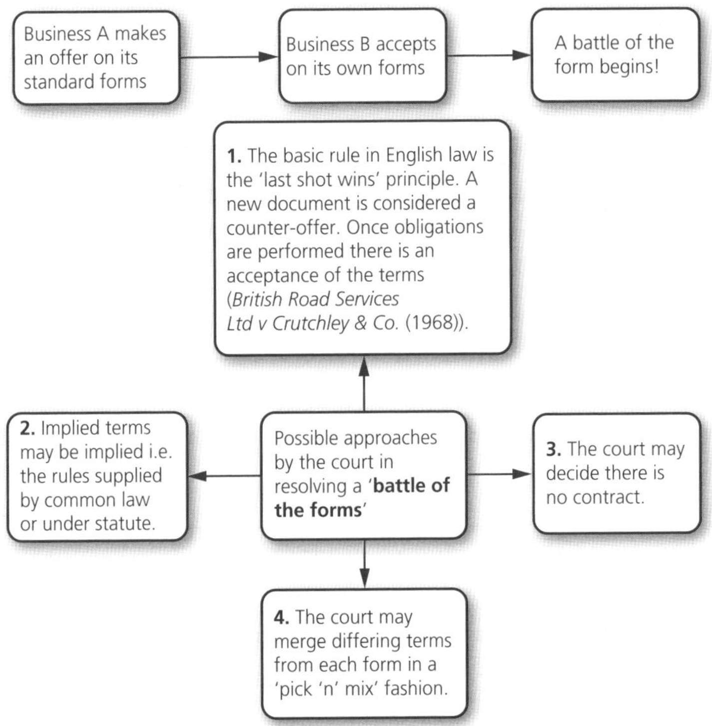

Case:	
***British Road Services Ltd v Crutchley & Co. Ltd* (1968)**	Facts: Crutchley took delivery of whiskey from BRS. The BRS driver gave Crutchley a delivery note containing their company's terms. This was stamped by Crutchley with the words, 'received under our conditions' before being handed back to the BRS driver. Held: The stamp by Crutchley was a counter-offer, which crucially BRS accepted when they handed over the whiskey.

- The 'last shot' approach was also adopted by the majority of the Court of Appeal in the leading decision, *Butler Machine Tool Co. Ltd v Ex-Cell-O Corporation (England) Ltd* (1979).
- This was also confirmed in *Tekdata Intercommunications v Amphenol Ltd* (2009).

Research Point

What was the range of alternate analyses given by Lord Denning MR in the minority in *Butler Machine Tool Co. Ltd v Ex-Cell-O Corporation (England) Ltd* (1979)? What are the advantages and disadvantages of his minority approach?

Checkpoint – revocation and acceptance

Item on checklist:	**Done!**
I can list the different ways an offer can be revoked or come to an end, and give case law examples	
I can define what makes an effective revocation	
I can state what amounts to acceptance and give examples	
I can define the different methods of acceptance	
I can state the rule relating to 'silence' when a party is presented with an offer	
I can state the 'postal rule'	
I can explain the statutory position relating to unsolicited goods and services	

Checkpoint – continued

Item on checklist:	Done!
I can explain the courts' approach to instantaneous communication methods	
I can define the 'last shot' principle and give case law examples of its use	

2.6 Intention to create legal relations

Agreements are made all the time, every day, and in all sorts of circumstances. They can involve not only offer, acceptance and consideration but also that the parties are bound by the terms of the agreement. Despite this the law freely accepts it is not always the case that parties intend to be legally accountable and able to sue for breach of contract should one of the parties not fulfil their obligations under the contract.

- The law therefore states there **must** be an intention to create legal relations for a contract to be legally binding.
- If all the parties engaged in negotiations, to all outward appearances, agree identical terms on an identical subject matter, an apparent intention to be bound may suffice (an objective test).
- Where there is no 'intention to create legal relations' there is no contract that can be legally enforceable.
- The courts have taken the following position:

Domestic and social agreements	Assumption that the parties do <u>NOT</u> intend to be legally bound	Can the assumption be rebutted? **YES**
Commercial and business transactions	Assumption that the parties <u>DO</u> intend their relationship to be legally binding	Can the assumption be rebutted? **YES**

- It is possible the above mentioned can be changed by the court should there be significant evidence to the contrary.

2.6.1 Domestic and/or social agreements

- The courts seem quite clear generally speaking when the matters relate to families.

Case:	
***Balfour v Balfour* (1919)**	Facts: A husband was working abroad and agreed to pay his wife an allowance of £30 per month because she was unable to accompany him. He failed to pay and the wife sued. Held: The action failed because not only was there a lack of consideration but the court was adamant the agreement was entirely domestic. The wife failed to provide evidence to rebut the presumption that there was no intention to create legal relations (a contract).
***Merritt v Merritt* (1970)**	A husband left his wife for another woman. He agreed to pay £40 to his former wife, per month, towards the repayment of the mortgage and once the mortgage was repaid he would transfer the house into her sole name. Once the mortgage was repaid, however, he refused to do this and the Court of Appeal was satisfied that there was an intention to legally bind.

Workpoint

In *Balfour v Balfour* (1919) and *Merritt v Merritt* (1970) the courts arrived at differing decisions despite both cases involving an agreement between husband and wife.

Why do you think this is?

- The automatic presumption is equally prevalent in social agreements, for example between friends. Equally, the courts are open to the presumption being rebutted should there be sufficient evidence.

Case:	
***Simpkins v Pays* (1955)**	Facts: A lodger shared a household with two others who were family members. Every week they entered a Sunday newspaper competition in the defendant's name with each of the three paying equal shares. One week the entry was successful but the defendant refused to pay the claimant, claiming there was no intention to create legal relations. Held: The mutual arrangement was a joint venture with the claimant rightly believing any prize would be shared.

Peck v Lateu (1973)	Two women agreed should either of them win at bingo then the winnings would be shared. It was held here that there was an intention to create legal relations.

- It would appear that the courts are happy to decide that there is an intention to create legal relations where there is an exchange of money or where someone risks their financial security.

2.6.2 Commercial and/or business agreements

Definition

Honourable pledge clause: A clause contained within a contract stipulating the contract has no legal basis and cannot be enforced. *Rose and Frank Co. v J R Crompton and Bros* (1925).

A letter of comfort: A letter by a party to a contact to another party stating an eagerness to enter into contractual obligations without the rudiments of a legally enforceable contract. *Kleinwort Benson Ltd v Malaysia Mining Corporation Bhd* (1989).

Subject to contract: An agreement that is not legally effective as a contract.

- It is widely assumed in commercial or business dealings that an agreement is intended to be legally binding unless there is significant evidence to the contrary and a different intention can be shown: *Esso Petroleum v Customs and Excise Commissioners* (1976).
- The principle also includes where prizes are offered in a competition and the competition is designed to promote the organisation offering the prize. The public can rely on the principle when entering competitions.
- Some parties state through a 'honourable pledge clause' that they have no intention of being legally bound as in *Rose and Frank Co. v J R Crompton and Bros* (1925).

Workpoint

What reasons did the court give for dismissing the action brought in *Kleinwort Benson Ltd v Malaysia Mining Corporation Bhd* (1989)?

Checkpoint – intention to create legal relations

Item on checklist:	Done!
I can state the presumption in respect of social and domestic arrangements	
I can state the presumption in respect of business and commercial transactions	
I can define an 'honourable pledge clause' providing a case example of its use	
I can define a 'letter of comfort' providing a case example of its use	

Potential exam questions

1) Bizhan wrote to Odele on Saturday offering 20 pairs of designer shoes at £30 per pair. Odele wrote back declaring that she was very much interested but asking two questions:

   a) Was there any extra charge for postage and packaging?

   b) Were the shoes genuine designer shoes?

   On Monday whilst on her lunch break Odele went into town to do some shopping. Realising just how expensive designer shoes were now in the shops, Odele emailed Bizhan when she got back to the office. The email stated, 'Accept your price of £30 per pair of shoes'.

   Assuming the shoes are genuine designer shoes, is there a contract? If yes, is delivery included in the price?

2) Lord Clarke confirms in the Supreme Court in the RTS case (2010):

   '...(2) Contracts may come into existence, not as a result of offer and acceptance, but during and as a result of performance.'

   Discuss.

3) Any acceptance, so long as it's communicated, is a valid acceptance.

   Discuss.

4) Joan was an antiques dealer of rare and fine items and had recently come into possession of a Louis XIV chandelier. Joan immediately thought of Lord and Lady Burns who lived in Hawthorn Manor. Lord and Lady Burns received a letter from Joan asking whether they would be interested in purchasing the chandelier for placement within Hawthorn Manor. Lord Burns wrote back to Joan, 'I will collect the chandelier from your shop on Saturday. For the chandelier I will pay £2,500 and unless I hear otherwise I will consider the chandelier mine and you are happy with the arrangements.'

   Advise Lord Burns on his legal position.

   a) Joan sold the Chandelier to Lord Bowen for £3,000 having ignored Lord Burns's letter.

   b) Lord Burns decided he no longer wanted to buy the chandelier yet Joan's delivery drivers had placed the chandelier on the delivery truck ready for delivery the next morning with a note, 'Sold to Lord Burns, ready for delivery'.

Chapter 3
Consideration

3.1 Introduction

- There are four essentials required to form a legally binding contract:
  - offer
  - acceptance
  - the intention to be legally bound, and
  - **consideration**.
- How consideration entered contract law is unclear but by the 17th century it was a requirement that there was a reason for a promise given.

3.2 Definition

- Consideration is giving a benefit or taking away a disbenefit.
- So should Adam sell his aeroplane to Daniel for £10,000, Daniel is getting the benefit of an aeroplane with the detriment of handing over £10,000 of his savings.
- Sir Frederick Pollock (1950) in *Principles of Contract Law* gave a succinct definition which is more like the modern commercial contract:

'An act or forbearance of one party, or the promise thereof, is the price for which the promise of the other is bought, and the promise thus given for value is enforceable'.

- The definition was confirmed in *Dunlop Pneumatic Tyre Co. Ltd v Selfridge and Co. Ltd* (1915) by the House of Lords.

Workpoint

Close your book and write a definition of consideration.

Definition

Executed consideration: This occurs where one party has 'executed' or 'carried out' their side of the bargain. The other party's consideration is pending completion and thus executory.

- It might be easiest to think of consideration as being something of value that is given in return for another's promise.
- With executed consideration there is a promise by one party in return for a promise by another party. Should one party fail to carry out a requirement of the contract they would be in breach of contract and might be subject to litigation.

Definition

Executory consideration: Concerns an agreement to carry out an act in the future.

- With an executed consideration there is no obligation on the party making the offer in a unilateral contract until the other party executes or performs their part of the agreement. Think rewards and *Carlill v Carbolic Smoke Ball Co. Ltd* (1893).

3.3 The rules of consideration

- The rules in their basic format are:

  1. Consideration need not be adequate but it must be sufficient.
  2. Consideration must move from the promisee (though not necessarily to the promisor).
  3. Consideration must not be in the past.
  4. Consideration will not be found if a party is legally obliged to do it.

3.3.1 Consideration need not be adequate but it must be sufficient

- The courts are not concerned with whether one side of a contractual agreement has paid too much or too little for something. It does not affect the validity of the contract.

- The general rule per Lord Denning MR in *Lloyds Bank Ltd v Bundy* (1975) is:

'no bargain will be upset which is the result of the ordinary interplay of forces.'

- A promise has no contractual enforceability unless *some* value has been given to it.

  Whether something is adequate is for the parties to decide. For example as long as there is no fraud, there would still be sufficient consideration where there was a contract for the sale of a world class footballer for a drawing pin, because there is an economic value attached to both items.

- A party may convert a gift or promise into a binding agreement by applying a nominal consideration.

Example: the granting of a lease at a 'peppercorn' (tiny) rent.

Case:	
***Thomas v Thomas* (1842)**	Despite nothing being mentioned in his will, a man before his death had expressed the wish that his wife should remain in their house. £1 a year in ground rent was charged by the executors of the will. The executors eventually tried, (and failed) to evict the wife. The wife had paid the ground rent and despite its small amount, it was nevertheless good consideration. Patterson J: *'consideration means some thing which is of some value in the eyes of the law, moving from the plaintiff: it may be of some benefit to the plaintiff, or some detriment to the defendant; but at all events it must be moving from the plaintiff. Now that which is suggested as the consideration here, a pious respect for the wishes of the testator, does not in any way move from the plaintiff; it moves from the testator; therefore, legally speaking, it forms no part of the consideration.'*

- Consideration must be sufficient. Therefore what is promised must:

  1. be tangible
  2. be real
  3. possess actual value.

- *White v Bluett* (1853) shows that it can be difficult to distinguish between what possesses value, is tangible or is indeed real.

Case:	
***White v Bluett* (1853)**	The court decided it was not good consideration for a son to refrain from pestering his father over the contents of a will in exchange for the cancelling of a debt. There was no economic value to the consideration. The court did not seek to define 'economic value' but did consider whether it was present.

- Interestingly in *Ward v Byham* (1956) a promise to keep a child happy was considered good consideration.

Case:	
***Chappell and Co. Ltd v Nestlé Co. Ltd* (1960)**	Nestlé ran a promotion to sell their chocolate. They offered records to the public for 1s 6d each plus three Nestlé chocolate bar wrappers. The wrappers were thrown away, but despite this the court held that the three wrappers were part of the consideration. *'A contracting party can stipulate for what consideration he chooses. A peppercorn does not cease to be good consideration if it is established that the promisee does not like pepper and will throw away the corn.' Lord Somerville*

3.3.2 Consideration must move from the promisee (though not necessarily to the promisor)

- If we use the example of Adam from 3.2 above, the consideration can be seen in diagram form below.

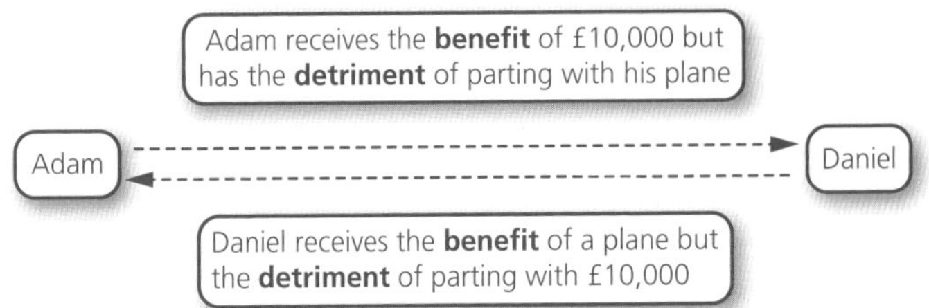

A party may only enforce an agreement if they have provided consideration. There has to be privity of contract. The promise cannot be enforced by a party that has not paid. (*Tweddle v Atkinson* (1861)).

Definition

Privity of contract: In order to sue or be sued in contract law a person or business must be privy (a party) to that contract.

Case:	
***Tweddle v Atkinson* (1861)**	The claimant's action failed. He was not a party to the contract despite the contract being made for his benefit since no consideration had moved away from him. In this case the claimant's father and father-in-law agreed to pay the claimant £300 collectively for consideration of the marriage.

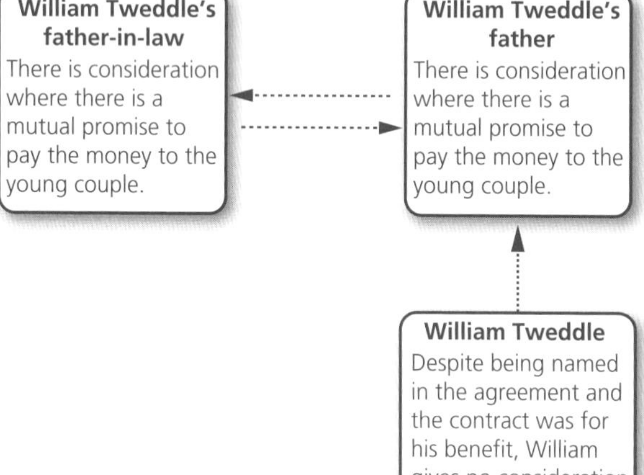

Workpoint

In *Tweddle v Atkinson* (1861) the claimant's action failed. Why would the claimant's father be more likely to have a successful action?

- The rule that consideration must move from the promisee is, like so many others, subject to exceptions.

Contract Law Act 1999 → Provides that as long as consideration has been given by someone, a third party may enforce a contract for his own benefit.

Case:	
***Shanklin Pier Ltd v Detel Products Ltd* (1951)**	A pier company contracted with another company to re-paint the pier. The contractors used a certain type of paint requested by the pier company on the basis that the manufacturers (the defendant) assured them it was able to withstand sea erosion and corrosion. When the paint proved ineffective the pier company was not able to bring an action against the contractors who had used the paint as requested. They were however able to sue the manufacturers (for the defective paint) even though they had no contract with them.

Workpoint

Robert is putting up a fence in his back garden. However, he has not ordered enough wood and gives Luciano £40 for some more. He also says that when he collects his scratchcard winnings he will give Luciano £15 towards the diesel he will use in collecting the wood from the garden centre. Luciano never receives the £15 towards the cost of diesel.

Advise Robert whether in respect of the £15 there is a legally enforceable agreement.

Workpoint

Neil is a season ticket holder at Leeds United. He wants his friend, Alex, to support them too and give up supporting Manchester United. Neil has told Alex that if he denounces his support for Manchester United and declares his allegiance to Leeds United, he will buy him a season ticket so they can go to the games together next season. Dismayed after Manchester lose to Leeds United 5-0 in a cup match Alex denounces his support for Manchester United, but when the new season ticket prices come out for Leeds United, because of promotion and a rise in prices, Neil is unable to buy Alex a season ticket and instead gives him a Leeds United mouse mat, pencil case and football.

Advise Alex whether he can claim a season ticket from Neil.

3.3.3 Consideration must not be past

Past consideration = no consideration

- Consideration must come after the agreement, otherwise it is a gratuity or gift.

  An example of past consideration could be where Tom fixes John's car while John is in hospital. John recovers and leaves hospital and is touched by Tom's kindness and promises to pay him £25. If John doesn't pay Tom, an action brought by Tom would fail. Past consideration = no consideration as we have seen, and Tom's fixing of John's car is past in relation to John's consideration to pay.

- The action in the example given fails because there is **no causal link**. The act of fixing the car was not made as a direct response to the promise of £25.

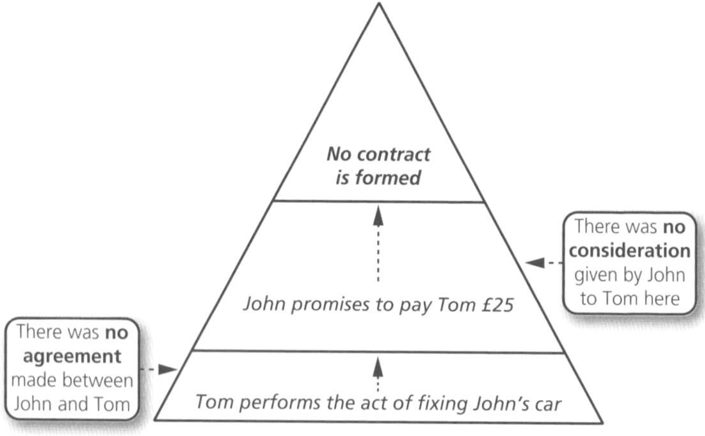

Important principle:

- Where there is an automatic expectation that something will be paid for, such as filling a car up with petrol, using a hotel room minibar, or eating a meal at a restaurant, the court will recognise and enforce this.

Case:	
***McArdle* (1951)**	The people moving into a property were asked to sign an agreement to repay the cost of repairs and improvements which had been made sometime before. The repairs had been made to the property before an agreement had been reached and therefore rendered the contract unenforceable.

***Roscorla v Thomas* (1842)**	The sale of a horse was agreed between the claimant and defendant. After the sale the claimant asked about the horse's temperament and was promised by the defendant that the horse was 'sound and free from vice'. However the opposite was true and the claimant tried to sue because of the defendant's promise. The court held that the action should fail. There was no consideration given for the promise.

Workpoint

Law Revision Comittee 1937 – *Sixth Interim Report on the 'The Statute of Frauds and the Doctrine of Consideration'*

The Law Revision Commitee recommended (unsuccessfully) in 1937 that the 'past consideration' rule be abolished.

Do you think it was right that the Law Revision Committee's recommendation to abolish the 'past consideration' rule was never adopted?

The **exception** to the rule is *Lampleigh v Braithwaite*.

Case:	
***Lampleigh v Braithwaite* (1615)**	Facts: A man had been killed by Braithwaite. Braithwaite asked Lampleigh to obtain a King's pardon for him. Braithwaite promised Lampleigh £100 in recognition of the considerable costs borne by him. The £100 was never paid. *Prima facie* Lampleigh's action should have failed because his efforts were 'past' in relation to Braithwaite's promise to pay. Held: despite there being no mention of payment at the time of Braithwaite's request to Lampleigh, it was obvious that a payment would have been in the minds of both parties and Braithwaite's request for a pardon contained an implied promise of the same. Therefore the 'request' and 'promise' were part of a continuing sequence of events and enforceable.

Research Point

Consider the judgment given by Bowen LJ in *Re Casey's Patents* (1892). Does this contradict or support the 'past consideration rule'?

Workpoint

Construct a diagram or flow chart that illustrates the exception to the rule stated in *Lampleigh v Braithwaite* (1615) as affirmed and restated in *Pao On v Lau Yiu Long* (1980).

Statutory exceptions to the rule

1. **Bills of Exchange Act 1882, s 27** – for a bill of exchange a previous debt will be good consideration.
2. **Limitation Act 1980, s 27(5)** – where debt is acknowledged by a debtor, for the intention of working out the beginning of the limitation period, the date of debt accruing shall be, not before, but from the date of the debt being acknowledged.

Research Point

Make a list of the conditions stipulated by Lord Scarman in *Pao On v Lau Yiu Long* (1980) that need to be applied in order for past consideration to be valid.

3.3.4 Consideration will not be found if a party is legally obliged to do it

- There is not good consideration where the claimant is bound by the provisions of an existing contractual obligation owed to the defendant or where a public duty is imposed by law. There is no new detriment.

Case:	
***Stilk v Myrick* (1809)**	Facts: A captain promised to pay the remaining sailors of a ship extra for sailing it back to port after two sailors had deserted. He broke this promise. Held: there was not good consideration because the sailors were contractually bound to sail the ship back to port anyway.

- However the cases of *Hartley v Ponsonby* (1857) and *Ward v Byham* (1956) show that regardless of a party being legally obliged to do something, there will be good consideration if a party in doing what they were legally bound to do goes above and beyond 'the call of duty'.
- This remains the general consensus and can be seen in *Glasbrook Bros Ltd v Glamorgan County Council* (1925).

Case:	
***Glasbrook Bros Ltd v Glamorgan County Council* (1925)**	The House of Lords held that despite the police being bound by public duty to protect the pit the fact that they provided more men than would have otherwise been the case meant there was good consideration for the promise.
***Reading Festival* (2006)**	The decision in *Glasbrook* was justified by the Court of Appeal in this case. *'The police are entitled to payment for providing special police services if requested to do so, "special police services" being broadly defined as those over and above their general obligation to maintain law and order and keep the peace.'*

- Matters were given a statutory footing by section 25(1) of the Police Act 1996.

> *'The chief officer of police of a police force may provide, at the request of any person, special police services at any premises or in any locality the police are for which the force is maintained, subject to the payment to the police authority of charges on such scales as may be determined by that authority.'*

Case:	
***Harris v Sheffield United Football Club* (1988)**	It was held that a large police presence to prevent large scale public disorder at a football ground was an extra service that went above and beyond the existing call of duty for the police.

- A duty duly performed to a third party may provide good consideration, *Scotson v Peggy* (1861).

Williams v Roffey Bros & Nicholls (Contractors) Ltd (1990)

The facts
- Roffey had a building contract to refurbish 27 flats and subcontracted the car pentry and joinery work to Williams.
- Williams suffered financial hardship and was struggling to satisfy the contract with Roffey.
- In order to avoid a late completion penalty from their client, Roffey offered Williams £10,300 to complete the work on time.
- Roffey failed to pay.

Held
- According to the Court of Appeal Williams was owed the money by Roffey.
- There was a contract.
- Where one party to a contract promises extra payment in return for a **new** benefit or the **avoidance** of a detriment there is a binding agreement.
- The extra commercial benefit to Roffey was not having to pay a late completion penalty to their client. The extra benefit was secured by the promise to pay Williams to complete the work on time (which in turn was their consideration to Roffey).

Quote
Glidewell LJ, sitting in the Court of Appeal: 'If A has entered into a contract with B to do work for, or to supply goods or services to, B in return for payment by B and at some stage before A has completely performed his obligations under the contract, B has reason to doubt whether A will, or will be able to, complete his side of the bargain and B thereupon promises A an additional payment in return for A's promise to perform his contractual obligations on time and as a result of giving his promise B obtains in practice a benefit, or obviates a disbenefit, and B's promise is not given as a result of economic duress or fraud on the part of A, then the benefit to B is capable of being consideration for B's promise, so that promise will be legally binding.'

Principle
Should party A and party B have a legally binding contract for A to provide B with goods or services and B becomes aware that A will not be able to satisfy their part of the contract, should B promise A an additional payment for satisfying the contract, it will be enforceable so long as:
1. The promise is not gained through economic duress or fraud by A.
2. There is an extra benefit to be received by B owing to the contract being completed.

Definition

Economic duress: The forcing of contract variation by one party in a commercial contract through the use of coercion or commercial pressure.

Research Point

State the facts *and* legal principles in the following cases:

- *Hartley v Ponsonby* (1857)
- *Collins v Godefroy* (1831)
- *Stilk v Myrick* (1809)
- *Glasbrook Bros v Glamorgan County Council* (1925)
- *Williams v Roffey Bros & Nicholls Contractors Ltd* (1990)
- New *Zealand Shipping Co. Ltd v A M Satterthwaite & Co. Ltd (The Eurymedon)* (1975)
- *Pao On v Lau Yiu Long* (1980)

3.4 Part payment of debt – the common law rule

Example: Hazel owes Ged £100 with the money being due on 14th October. Hazel promises to pay (or pays) £50 as long as Ged promises to forgo the remaining balance. Is Hazel able to enforce the agreement?

Sir Guenter Treitel (2010) in *The Law of Contract* states:

'The general rule at common law is that a creditor is not bound by an undertaking to accept part payment in full settlement of a debt. An accrued debt can be discharged only by accord and satisfaction. A promise by the debtor to pay part of the debt provides no consideration for the accord, as it is merely a promise to perform part of an existing duty owed to the creditor.'

- Unless it is supported by a new consideration or deed, part payment of a debt on its due date does not discharge the whole debt, regardless of the creditor's promise to forgo the unpaid amount. This is known and referred to as 'Pinnels rule' or 'The rule in *Pinnel's case*' (1602).
- So at common law, in the example above, despite paying (or promising to pay) £50 to Ged, Hazel will still owe the remaining balance to Ged even if Ged were to forgo the rest of what Hazel owed him.
- *Foakes v Beer* (1884) affirmed the 'common law rule'.

Case:	
***Foakes v Beer* (1884)**	Mrs Beer agreed that Foakes could pay her £2,090 in installments after a court ruled against Foakes. If the debt was paid by the agreed date, Mrs Beer agreed not to take further action. Foakes refused to pay when Mrs Beer later requested interest, to which she was entitled. In applying 'Pinnel's rule' Mrs Beer was successful.

Case:	
***D C Builders v Rees* (1965)**	D C Builders were at the point of going out of business. They were owed £482 for the balance of work that they had completed. Rees offered to pay £300 in a final settlement of the debt. D C Builders reluctantly accepted. The builders successfully brought an action for the remaining balance despite having agreed to accept less.

- Whilst there is widespread support of the rule, this support is not unconditional.

For	Against
The House of Lords in *Foakes v Beer* (1884)	Law Revision Committee, Sixth Interim Report on **'The Statute of Frauds and the Doctrine of Consideration'** (1937) Cmd 5449 recommended the ending of the rule
The majority of the Court of Appeal in *D & C Builders v Rees* (1966)	In an article the Former Chair of the Law Commission, Dame Mary Arden, commented that the rule was ridiculous [1997] CLJ 516
Followed by the Court of Appeal in *Re Selectmove* (1995)	
Janet O'Sullivan article 'In Defence of Foakes v Beer' [1996] CLJ 219-28	

Workpoint

What is the fundamental difference between *Hartley v Ponsonby* (1857) and *Stilk v Myrick* (1809)?

3.4.1 Part payment of debt – exceptions to the rule

As mentioned above the idea of a 'fresh consideration' (a new benefit and new detriment) is an exception to the rule. Some other exceptions can be seen below.

1. *Early payment* – Should the creditor request payment sooner and promise to forgo the remaining debt, this will be regarded as a fresh consideration. So if Ged requests £50 from Hazel on 8th October and promises to forgo the remaining balance, this will be a fresh consideration.
2. *Accepting something other than money as part payment or in conjunction with money as part payment* – The acceptance of a new football shirt instead of money, or a new football shirt with £30, will be good consideration for the settlement of the debt whether or not the shirt and/or money have the same value as the original debt.
3. *Hirachand Punamchand v Temple* (1911) – It was held that when the **uncle** of a debtor paid a lesser sum, this was full settlement of the debt. Therefore it is not possible for a creditor to sue the original debtor where part payment has been made by a third party.
4. *Composition agreements* – If there are many creditors who are owed money by the same debtor, they may agree to accept a proportion or percentage of what they are owed as a full and final settlement of the original monies owed.

3.4.2 The doctrine of promissory estoppel

Definition

Estoppel: The barring or denying of a party from affirming a particular claim (or fact) inconsistent with a previous position that a party took, through words or conduct, especially where a representation has been acted or relied upon by others.

- If a claim is made by a creditor for an outstanding balance, the debtor will have the defence of promissory estoppel. Promissory estoppel prevents a creditor going back on a previous promise.
- The doctrine was developed by Lord Denning in *Central London Property Trust Ltd v High Trees House Ltd* (1947) and *Combe v Combe* (1951).

Case:	
***Central London Property Trust Ltd v High Trees House Ltd* (1947)**	The defendants had leased flats from the claimants which in turn were subsequently sub-let. Because of the outbreak of World War II the flats remained largely unoccupied which meant the defendants were unable to pay the rent to the claimants. The claimants allowed the defendants to pay a reduced rent until the war ended. By the end of World War II the flats were fully occupied and the claimants brought an action for the rent arrears at the original cost for the last two quarters. The defendants had relied on the promise for an extensive period of time and thus were able to rely on estoppel to prevent the claimants going back on their promise.

- The doctrine of promissory estoppel was given a more succinct definition in *Combe v Combe* (1951) by Lord Denning:

'Where one party has, by his words or conduct, made to the other a promise or assurance which was intended to affect the legal relations between them and to be acted on accordingly, then, once the other party has taken him at his word and acted upon it, the one who gave the promise or assurance cannot afterwards be allowed to revert to the previous legal relations as if no such promise or assurance had been made by him.'

- Applying the more accurately measured definition of promissory estoppel given by Lord Denning in *Combe v Combe* to *Central London*, from 1940 onwards they would obviously be estopped from claiming the rent arrears.

Research Point

What was the consequence of *Re Selectmove* (1995)?

3.5 Summary

- 'An act or forbearance of one party, or the promise thereof, **is the price for which the promise of the other is bought**, and the promise thus given for value is enforceable.'
- The definition was confirmed in *Dunlop Pneumatic Trye Co. Ltd v Selfridge and Co. Ltd* (1915) by the House of Lords.

- Consideration may not be in the past but it may be executed or executory.
- Consideration must move from the promisee although not necessarily to the promisor.
- Whilst not necessarily adequate, consideration must be sufficient (real, tangible and with value).
- For a person to be sued they must have given consideration under the contract.
- Performance of existing obligations or public duties and part-payment of debt will not amount to good consideration unless under certain circumstances.

Checkpoint – consideration

Item on checklist:	**Done!**
I can give a definition of consideration	
I can define executory consideration and executed consideration	
I can list the rules of consideration and use case law to illustrate them	
I can explain past consideration and how it can be justified	
I understand the exception in *Lampleigh v Braithwaite* (1615)	
I can define the exception to the basic rule of consideration and the performance of existing duties	
I can list the principles from *Williams v Roffey* (1990)	
I can explain 'Pinnel's rule' and the exceptions to the rule	

Potential exam questions

1) The courts are prepared to accept that consideration for a new agreement could be provided by the performance of an existing duty.

   Is this an accurate assessment of the courts' approach? Discuss.

2) Lorimer is having a new garage built by Sniffer Clarke Ltd. Bremner Building Co., in a separate contract, agrees with Lorimer to carry out the excavation work needed for the building of Lorimer's new garage. Bremner Building Co. and Lorimer agree on a price of £6,000. They both understand that the work will cost substantially more; however Lorimer and the managing director of Bremner Building Co., Billy, are old school friends.

   When Bremner Building Co. begins excavating, they quickly realise the job is bigger than they had anticipated and this means they will need more equipment which will take time to obtain. Having discussed the matter with Lorimer, Lorimer offers Bremner Building Co. an extra £1,000 to finish the work on time. When the work is finished, Lorimer is only prepared to pay £6,000.

   a) What advice would you give Bremner Building Co.?
   b) How would your answer be different if the £1,000 had been promised by Sniffer Clarke Ltd because of a waiting list of other jobs?

3) What criticisms could be made of judicial developments in the rule, 'consideration need not be adequate but it must be sufficient'?

Chapter 4
Contract terms

4.1 Introduction

Being able to distinguish what the parties have agreed to through the process of negotiation is one of the most important aspects of contracts. This is true of a written document or a verbal agreement.

- The terms agreed upon and written down or verbally agreed can be considered **express terms** to the contract.
- The other terms may be **implied terms**.
- **Implied terms** may occur in the following circumstances:
  1. Where the court considers the parties to the contract would have included the term but for a misunderstanding or genuine mistake.
  2. Where the commercial value of the contract depends on it.

4.2 Representations

Definition

Representations: Statements made at the pre-contractual stage.

- Pre-contractual representations only create contractual obligations if they are terms of the agreement that the parties have agreed to be bound by. Certain representations and statements are not terms and the court will not seek to enforce these.

1) Representation	This is a true statement of fact designed to tempt the opposite party to contract but not intended to form the basis or part of the contract. There is **no** contractual obligation. However despite the representation not forming part of the contract if the representation is false then remedies may be awarded as a result of an action brought for **misrepresentation**.

2) Opinions	An opinionated statement is not based on facts and as such carries no legal weight, unless of course the author of the statement knows it is false (*Bisset v Wilkinson* (1927), *Esso Petroleum Co Ltd v Marden* (1976)).
3) Trade puffs	These are representations or statements that no person would or could take seriously because of their frivolous nature. They are a tactic used in marketing designed to increase sales, e.g. the 'Lynx effect' or the 'Carlsberg … probably' campaigns. Should the Lynx effect not work or Carlsberg not be the best lager in the world no action in contract is available.

Case	
***Bisset v Wilkinson* (1927)**	The Privy Council held that a statement by a vendor that a plot of land could support 2,000 sheep was no more than an honest opinion. The vendor was not experienced enough to make such a statement about whether the land was sufficient for sheep farming.
***Esso Petroleum Co. Ltd v Marden* (1976)**	Where a party gives a false opinion, knowingly or not, and they are an expert in that particular field, the party to whom the statement was made may bring an action for remedies.

4.3 Express terms

- The difference between a term and representation is the legal consequence attached to it. Parties have the right to sue if a statement that has been incorporated into the contract as a term is breached. It is generally straightforward to decide whether a statement or express term has been incorporated into a contract if it is written. If a term is oral, the courts have devised guidelines to decide whether the statement is a term of a contract or not.

> *The rule – Whether a statement is a term of a contract depends on the court. Considering what the 'reasonable man' would assume to be in the minds of the parties at the time the contract was formed.*

- To help the application of this test, several factors have been developed by the courts for consideration. These are:

1. The importance of the statement/representation.
2. Special knowledge and skill.
3. The timing of the statement.
4. The reduction into writing of the contract.
5. The extent to which the term is drawn to the other party's attention.

1. *The importance of the statement/representation*

Should a statement be so important that but for its inclusion a party would not have agreed the contract, then it is highly probable the statement is a term.

Case:	
***Birch v Paramount Estates (Liverpool) Ltd* (1956)**	A promise was made by property developers that a home being bought by a newly-wed couple would be as good as the show home they had seen. This was not the case and the Court of Appeal held that the statement was effectively the nucleus of the agreement and was the reason the couple entered into the contract with the property developers.

2. *Special knowledge and skill*

Should a person claiming to be an expert in a particular field or possessing specialist knowledge make a statement, this is more likely to be seen as being part of a contract.

Case:	
***Oscar Chess Ltd v Williams* (1957)**	Williams sold Oscar a car which he genuinely believed was a 1948 Morris 10. The car registration documents confirmed this. The car was later discovered to be a 1939 model and Oscar sued unsuccessfully for breach of warranty. Applying the reasonable man objective test it is clear the statement was not a term because the reasonable man would not have thought that Williams, who had no expertise or specialist skill and was relying completely on the registration documents, could have guaranteed the truth of the statement made.

	'One final word ... [the motor dealers only checked the log book] eight months later. They are experts, and, not having made that check at the time, I do not think they should now be allowed to recover against the innocent seller who produced to them all the evidence he had, namely, the registration book ... '. **Denning LJ**

3. *The timing of the statement*

In deciding whether a statement is a representation or term of a contract the court will consider the time difference between the making of the statement and the formation of the contract.

The longer the time difference between the two, the less likely a party will be able to claim that the statement was a term of the contract.

Case:	
***Routledge v McKay* (1954)**	Facts: After first being registered in 1939 a new registration book for a motorcycle wrongly gave the date as 1941. In 1949 the owner, as per the registration book, confirmed the date of registration as 1941 when contracting for the sale of the motorcycle with a potential buyer. When the buyer bought the motorcycle there was no mention in the written agreement of the motorcycle's age. The buyer tried to sue for a breach of warranty and failed. Held: the time lapse was too great between the negotiations and the sale between the buyer and seller for there to be a relationship between the two.

4. *The reduction into writing of the contract*

The court can draw an inference from an oral agreement that has or has not been put in writing. For example, where a statement is made orally but there is no written evidence, the court may infer from this that it was not intended to be a term of the agreement but was in fact a mere representation.

In *Routledge* there was no mention of the age of the car in the written agreement. The court inferred from this that if it was that important it would have been included.

5. *The extent to which the term is drawn to the other party's attention*

A term will not be seen to be incorporated into a contract until the other party receives notice of it.

Research Point

What are the facts of *O'Brien v MGN Ltd* (2001)? Which of the five factors above is it most applicable to?

Workpoint

Felippe is a collector and dealer of Egyptian archaeological artefacts. He buys a small Tutankhamen statue for £2,000 from Fernando who is selling off the family heirlooms after the death of his father. Felippe asks Fernando about its history and Fernando replies, 'Well I'm no expert but I think my father said he bought it at auction from the National Museum of Egyptian History'. Felippe later discovers the statue was not bought from the National Museum of Egyptian History at auction but at a collectors' conference and is only worth £250. Has a term been incorporated into the contract?

4.4 The 'parol evidence' rule

Definition

Parol evidence rule: Oral and/or intrinsic evidence is not admissable to add, vary or contradict a written contract.

- The rule preserves the sanctity of the written contract, and logically assumes that had something been very important when negotiations were taking place it would have been laid down in writing.
- Like so many rules in contract law there are exceptions:
  1. *Webster v Cecil* (1861) – Part of a written document stated that the price was £1,250. It was clear from the negotiations that this amount was inaccurate. The court allowed the alteration of the contract to show the true intentions of both parties.
  2. *Custom* – Terms may be implied into the contract where the parties are used to their application, for example by trade custom.
  3. *Where a contract cannot be performed until a specified event occurs* – This is best illustrated by *Pym v Campbell* (1856) where there was a written contract between the parties that was suspended by oral agreement until the subject of the contract had been verified by a third party. The court held the oral evidence showed the suspension of the contract was admissible.

4. *Invalidation* – Oral or verbal evidence will be permitted where one party disputes the validity of the contract on the grounds of mistake, misrepresentation or capacity.
5. *The written agreement is one part of a larger agreement* – Where a written contract is just one part of a larger agreement the parol evidence rule will not apply. The oral and verbal representations are as important as the written ones contained within the contract because they are a reflection of the parties' intentions.

Case:	
***J Evans & Son (Portsmouth) Ltd v Andrea Merzario Ltd* (1976)**	An oral assurance was given that machinery would be stored below deck to prevent rust. An error meant that in actual fact the machinery was not only stored on deck but also fell into the sea. The Court of Appeal held the oral assurance as admissible given the standard forms that had been used.

6. *Collateral contracts*

Case:	
***City and Westminster Properties (1934) v Mudd* (1958)**	Facts: the claimant had rented his shop to the defendant for six years. The claimant was well aware that the defendant was using the room next to the shop as sleeping quarters. A clause stating the use of the shop was limited to 'showrooms, workrooms and offices only' was inserted into the lease when it came up for renewal. As the clause prevented the use of the sleeping quarters, the defendant verbally agreed that he could still use the sleeping quarters and on this basis signed the written agreement. An action was brought for breach of covenant after the defendant used the sleeping quarters. Held: Even though it conflicted with the written agreement to only use the 'showrooms, workrooms and offices', the oral agreement was considered a collateral contract and the defendant was therefore able to use it in his defence to the action for breach of covenant.

Workpoint

A party's decision to contract can often be based on statements made during pre-contractual negotiations. How would a court come to a decision about whether such statements are mere representations or terms of the contract?

Workpoint

What are the pitfalls of not having a contract in writing?

4.5 Warranties, conditions and innominate terms

1. Terms, whether express or implied, have varying degrees of importance attached to them, depending on whether they are warranties, conditions or innominate terms.

	Description	Effect of a breach	Case
Condition	A condition is a term that goes to the very heart of a contract. Thus a very important term will be considered a condition	1) Repudiation (termination) of the contract and 2) Damages	*Poussard v Spiers and Pond* (1876)
Warranty	A warranty is considered to be less important than a condition. It is supplementary to the main crux of the contract	1) Damages only	*Bettini v Gye* (1876)
Innominate Term	Where the importance of a term is not expressed by the parties, implied by statute (section 15A Sale of Goods Act 1979) or judicial decision the term will be considered an innominate term	1) The court will decide upon a remedy once the affect of the breach has been considered	*Hong Kong Fir Shipping Co. Ltd v Kawasaki Kisen Kaisha Ltd* (1962)

Research Point

What are the facts of *Poussard v Spiers and Pond* (1876) and *Bettini v Gye* (1876)?

What were the reasons given by the courts for their decisions?

1. In *Hong Kong Fir Shipping Co. Ltd v Kawasaki Kisen Kaisha Ltd* (1962) the Court of Appeal said that some contractual terms are too problematic to be classified as a condition or warranty.
2. The breaching of wide ranging terms, such as something being 'fit for purpose', may have either large or small consequences which can only be known once a breach has occurred. Such terms are referred to as **innominate** terms.

4.6 Implied terms

- As well as express terms, implied terms may constitute part of a contract. There are three types:

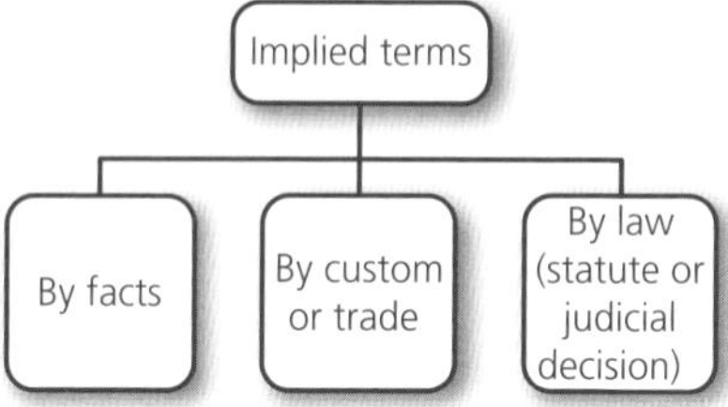

4.6.1 Terms implied by fact

- Terms implied by fact are deduced from the intentions of the parties. They are seen to be so obvious that either they were not referred to because they were so obvious or they were left out by an innocent mistake.
- There are two tests:

1. The 'officious bystander' test as expressed by MacKinnon LJ in *Shirlaw v Southern Foundries (1926) Ltd* (1939):

   '*Prima facie* that which in any contract is left to be implied and need not be expressed is something so obvious that it goes without saying; so that if, while the parties were making their bargain an officious bystander were to suggest some express provision for it in their agreement, they would testily suppress him with a common "Oh of course".'

- Both parties have to be aware of the term and the test will only apply if both parties would have agreed to the term if it had been discussed.

Case:	
***Spring v National Amalgamated Stevedores and Dockers Society* (1956)**	Here the union argued that a term should be implied into the contract that there must be compliance with the 'Bridlington Agreement' (which governs the rules relating to members transferring between unions). The court rejected this view and said that, had an officious bystander been asked about the Bridlington Agreement, the member would not have said, 'of course' but would have asked what it was.
***Shell (UK) Ltd v Lostock Garages Ltd* (1976)**	The Court of Appeal refused an application by the claimant to have a term implied into the contract that Shell would not discriminate against the claimant by selling petrol and oil at a lower price to other garages. The court said that Shell would never have agreed to such a term.

Workpoint

What are the advantages and disadvantages of the 'officious bystander' test?

Research Point

In *Liverpool City Council v Irwin* (1976) when did Lord Denning suggest terms should be implied?

Did the House of Lords approve or reject his approach?

What did Lord Cross say?

2. The 'Business Efficacy' test

- Lord Wright in *Luxor (Eastbourne) Ltd v Cooper* (1941) stated a term to be one:

'of which it can be predicted that "it goes without saying", some term not expressed but necessary to give the transaction such business efficacy as the parties intended'.

- Where it is claimed by a party that a term should be implied in order to ensure business efficacy, the business efficacy test will be applied.
- The test made its debut in the leading case, *The Moorcock* (1889):

Case:	
***The Moorcock* (1889)**	Facts: The defendants owned a wharf on the Thames with a jetty and allowed the claimant, upon receipt of a landing charge, to keep his ship there ('The Moorcock'). Both parties knew when they agreed the contract that during low tide the Moorcock could be grounded, especially given its size. The claimant sued for the cost of repairing the ship when it suffered damage from being grounded at low tide. Held: The Court of Appeal held that the owner of the wharf taking reasonable steps to determine the state of anchorage and thus prevent damage to the ship was an implied term. This was despite the defendants claiming they had given no express assurances over the safety of the ship. Bowen LJ: *'In business transactions such as this, what the law desires to effect by the implication is to give such business efficacy to the transaction as must have been intended at all events by both parties who are businessmen.'*

4.6.2 Terms implied by custom or trade usage

- A term can be implied if there is evidence that it is local custom or trade usage. It should be noted that implied terms are an exception to the 'parol evidence rule'.
- In *Hutton v Warren* (1836) it was held by the court that a lease must be viewed in light of the local custom of a tenant receiving an allowance for seed and labour once the lease was terminated.
- Implied terms, and therefore custom, should not contradict express terms. However, they may add to them. Given this inconsistency the courts will only judge a party to be bound by the term if they knew about it.

- A custom which is reasonable and not contradictory to the express terms will bind both parties whether or not they knew about it.

Case	
***Les Affreteurs SA v Walford (Walford's Case)* (1919)**	If a custom had been accepted it would have contradicted the clause in the contract, and so it was held by the court to not be implied into the contract

- *British Crane Hire Corp. Ltd v Ipswich Plant Hire Ltd* (1975) confirmed this. Here, terms may also be implied into a contract by trade usage.

Case	
***British Crane Hire Corp. Ltd v Ipswich Plant Hire Ltd* (1975)**	The owner's terms of the crane hire were the trade norm and were thus implied into the contract even though they were not communicated at the time the contract was being agreed.

Workpoint

There are different kinds of implied terms, what are they?

Workpoint

What is the 'officious bystander' test and when may it **not** be used?

4.6.3 Terms implied by common law and by statute law

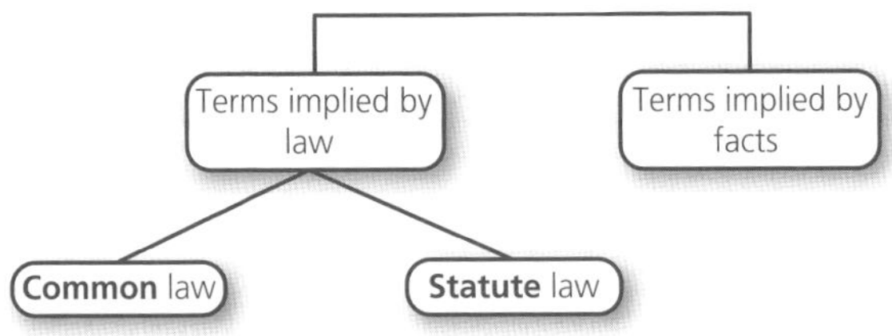

Terms are implied by law in two ways:

- Terms implied by law are implied into a contract regardless of the intentions or wishes of the parties. This is in contrast to terms implied by fact, which are implied because they are taken to be the intention of the parties.

- Where a judge implies a term into a contract because it is right to do so in the circumstances, and there are no routes in statute law, the case will act as precedent to future cases of a similar nature (*Liverpool City Council v Irwin* (1976)).
- There are various statutory provisions that have been introduced to redress the balance of power and provide consumers with protection when negotiating the sale of goods and the supply of services. These are:

  1. Sale of Goods Act 1979
  2. Supply of Goods and Services Act 1982

- Both Acts were subject to amendment by the Sale and Supply of Goods Act 1994. Specifically the substitution of a **new s 14(2) into the 1979 Act** and a **new s 4(2) into the 1982 Act**, implying a condition that instead of being **merchantable quality**, goods must be of a **satisfactory quality**.

4.6.3.1 Sale of Goods Act 1979 and terms implied under it

- *S 12 – Terms implied as to title*

Under this section a person selling the goods has the right to pass on the title to them, *Roland v Divall* (1923).

- *S 13 – Implied condition as to description*

There is an implied condition that the goods sold must correspond to the description applied to them by the seller. The section is particularly prevalent in contracts entered into where the buyer and seller do not meet face-to-face, for example when buying over the Internet or from catalogues.

Case:	
***Beale v Taylor* (1967)**	A car was advertised as a 'Herald convertible, white, 1961, twin carbs'. In reality the car was two halves welded together with only the rear end of the car matching the seller's description of the car. Despite not knowing the real history of the car the seller was nevertheless liable. Whilst the buyer had seen the car the court was in no doubt that he had also relied on the description given by the seller. **Had he not relied on the description given by the seller there would not have been a breach of s 13.**

***Harlingdon & Leinster Enterprises Ltd v Christopher Hull Fine Art Ltd* (1990)**	Slade LJ: *'If there was no such reliance by the purchaser, this may be powerful evidence that the parties did not contemplate that the authenticity of the description should constitute a term of the contract; in other words, that they contemplated that the purchaser would be buying the goods "as they were".'*

- *S 14(2) – implied condition as to the satisfactory quality of the goods*

Section 14(2) only applies where goods are sold, 'in the course of business' and not where private sales are concerned.

Under the 1979 Act goods should be of 'merchantable quality', a term defined in s 14(6) as meaning fit for purpose. Merchantable quality under the 1979 Act was changed to 'satisfactory quality' by s 1 of the **Sale and Supply of Goods Act 1994**.

'Satisfactory' is defined in s 14(2A) of the 1979 Act:

> *'Goods are of satisfactory standards if they meet the standard that a reasonable person would regard as satisfactory, taking account of any description of the goods, the price, (if relevant) and all other relevant circumstances.'*

Section 14 (2B) lists the following factors that can be taken into account when deciding whether goods are of a satisfactory quality:

1. Fitness for purpose for which goods of the same kind are normally supplied
2. Appearance/finish
3. Freedom from minor defects
4. Durability
5. Safety

Case:	
***Bartlett v Sidney Marcus* (1965)**	Facts: A second hand car was bought and after 300 miles the clutch failed. It was pointed out at the time of the sale that the clutch might need some work but it was claimed that the car was roadworthy in all other aspects. Held: the car was of 'satisfactory' quality and fit for purpose despite the clutch problem being more serious than originally thought.

If a higher price is paid, higher quality can be expected, *Clegg v Andersson* (2003).

Under s 14(2C) goods cannot be claimed to be unsatisfactory if:

1. The goods have been examined by the buyer and the defect is one which should have been discovered.
2. The defect is brought to the buyer's attention.

Research Point

Is it the case that when assessing merchandise standards considerations of safety are taken into account? Consider *Shine v General Guarantee Corporation* (1988).

- *S 14(3) – implied condition that the goods are fit for purpose*

A condition is implied into contracts that goods are fit for purpose where the buyer makes it known to the seller that the goods are required for a certain purpose. Should the seller sell for the purpose specified by the buyer and the goods are not fit for purpose there will be a breach.

Case:	
***Griffiths v Peter Conway* (1939)**	A lady contracted dermatitis from a new tweed coat she had purchased. Her not fit for purpose action failed because she had failed to mention her unusually sensitive skin.

This would not be the case where the buyer has not relied on the judgement or skill of the seller or where it would not be reasonable for him to do so.

Workpoint

Jenson aged 9 bought a go-kart from Lewis at 'Super Boys Toys' shop. When Jenson drove the go-kart outside his house, a wheel fell off and he crashed into a tree. Jenson suffered a broken arm as a result.

Under what sections of the Sale of Goods Act 1979/Sale and Supply of Goods Act 1994 could Lewis be liable?

- *S 15 – implied condition a sample of good should match the goods sold*

Three conditions are implied into a contract where the sale is based upon a sample:

1. The goods received must correspond to the sample.
2. The buyer must be afforded the opportunity to compare the sample with the bulk.
3. There must not be any unsatisfactory defects in the goods received that would have been noticed upon inspection of the sample.

4.6.3.2 Supply of Goods and Services Act 1982

Many of the implied terms in the Supply of Goods and Services Act 1982 mirror those found in the Sale of Goods Act 1979 as amended by the Sale and Supply of Goods Act 1994, namely:

1. title – s 2
2. description – s 3
3. satisfactory quality and fitness for purpose – s 4
4. sample – s 5.

There are other significant implied terms under the Supply of Goods and Services Act 1982 which are important for the supply of services.

- *S 13 – an implied term is included in the contract that the supplier of a service, acting in the course of business, will carry out the service with reasonable care and skill*

A person who has requested a service is entitled to expect that the supplier of the service or the person carrying out the service is duly qualified and will do so with both care and skill. Failing to do this will amount to a breach of the implied term.

Case:	
***Lawson v Supasink Ltd* (1984)**	The defendants were contracted to design, install and fit a kitchen for £1,200. The claimants sued and were able to claim their money back under s 13 after the defendants failed to follow the plans properly and produced shoddy work.

- *S 14 – if the contract does not specify a time frame for the service to be carried out, there is an implied term that the service will be carried out within a reasonable time.*

This is a question of fact and is based on the circumstances.

- *S 15 – where the consideration under the contract is not determined, the party in receipt of the service will have to pay a reasonable charge.*

This is also a question of fact. A price may not have been set when the parties were contracting; nevertheless the party receiving the service should expect to pay a reasonable charge.

Research Point

The Consumer Protection (Distance Selling) Regulations 2000 operate by including a number of implied terms into contracts which the seller must comply with for the transaction to be valid. The implied terms seek to protect the consumer. What are they?

Checkpoint – terms

Item on checklist:	**Done!**
I can state the difference between representations, opinions and trade puffs	
I can explain the difference between a term and a representation	
I can define the 'parol evidence' rule	
I can define the exceptions to the 'parol evidence' rule	
I can list the factors that determine whether a statement becomes a term	
I can explain the difference between conditions, warranties and innominate terms with cases to support each one	
I can explain the three different ways terms may be implied into a contract with case examples	
I can state the two different ways terms may be implied by law with case examples	

Potential exam question

A party's decision to contract can often be based on statements made during pre–contractual negotiations. How would a court come to a decision as to whether such statements are mere representations or terms of the contract?

Chapter 5

Misrepresentation

5.1 Introduction

Definition

Misrepresentation: A false statement of fact that persuades another party to enter into a contract.

- Some statements may form terms of the contract and therefore have legal significance. If they are breached there is the potential for legal action.
- Where it is stated factually and accurately, a mere representation that is not incorporated into a contract will have no legal significance. **However** there may be an action for misrepresentation if the representation is made falsely to persuade another party to enter the contract.
- Should an action for misrepresentation be successful, the remedies available are damages and rescission.

Definition

Rescission: Setting the contract aside.

5.2 The meaning of misrepresentation

1. A false statement of fact.
2. The representation must be by words or conduct.
3. The misrepresentation must be made before or at the time of the contract.
4. The statement must be made by one (the representor) to another (the representee) either directly or indirectly and where both become parties to the contract.

5. The representation must have been a false statement of fact that induced a party to enter into a contract.

1. A *false statement of fact*

- Examples:

  i. 'The dinner shirt is machine-washable'.
  ii. 'The artefacts have been fully restored'.
     - These are clearly statements of fact and if they are false they would be actionable as misrepresentation. Statements of honest opinions mistakenly held or future intentions are not usually actionable misrepresentations.

Case	
***Bisset v Wilkinson* (1927)**	During the sale of land, a representation was made that the land could support up to 2,000 sheep. The statement was made by the vendor, who was well aware that the land had never been used for sheep farming before. The court held there was no misrepresentation. What was said was just a **statement of opinion**.

- It is possible that the intention to do something in the future might be included as a term of a contract and a consideration. The failure of a party to carry this out would be a breach of contract. There could be no action for breach of contract or misrepresentation in respect of representations about future conduct because such statements cannot be statements of fact. However a **statement of intention** is actionable as a misrepresentation if it persuades a party to enter into a contract and there is evidence to suggest the maker of the statement knew the promise would never be kept.
- In respect of **silence as a misrepresentation of fact** the general rule is that if a party remains silent this does not amount to a misrepresentation. This rule has its roots in the legal maxim '*caveat emptor*' (let the buyer beware) and was confirmed by the House of Lords in *Hamilton v Allied Domecq Plc* (2007).

The rule is subject to the following exceptions:	Key case	Explanation
Half-truths	*Nottingham Patent Brick and Tile Co.v Butler* (1886) See also *Dimmock v Hallett* (1866)	A statement that is misleading because it does not accurately portray the truth may be regarded as a misrepresentation. In *Nottingham Patent Brick* a solicitor said that he was not aware of any restrictive covenants. This was correct but only because the solicitor had failed to carry out the appropriate checks.
Changes in circumstances	*With v O'Flannagan* (1936)	Where a true representation becomes false, a duty of disclosure in respect of the change of circumstances arises. In *With* a potential buyer of a medical practice was told the practice was worth £2,000 per annum. However when the contract was signed nearly five months later the practice was worth next to nothing due to the ill health of the vendor. The court decided there was a duty to disclose and thus the buyer had a right to revoke the contract.
Contracts that are *uberrimae fidei* –'of utmost good faith'	*Pan Atlantic Insurance Co. Ltd v Pine Top Insurance Co Ltd* (1995)	A duty to disclose will arise where one party is in a strong position to know the truth. A contract of insurance is an example of a contract of utmost good faith where there is an obligation on the insured to disclose, whether or not it is requested, all information relating to circumstances that could affect the contract. In such a contract it would not be reasonable to expect the insured to know all the details relevant to the provision of insurance.

Definition

Caveat emptor: Let the buyer beware.

Uberrimae fidei: Of utmost good faith.

Workpoint

How does the decision of *Bisset v Wilkinson* (1927) compare to that of *Smith v Land & House Property Corp.* (1885)?

How did the court differentiate between opinion and fact in these cases?

2. *The representation must be made in writing or by conduct*

- A false statement of fact may be made by conduct.

Case	
***Spice Girls Ltd v Aprilla World Service BV* (2000)**	Facts: The Spice Girls all appeared in promotions and marketing of Aprilla's scooters and motorbikes. The band knew that Geri Halliwell intended to leave and thus would be unable to fulfil the sponsorship deal. Held: The Court of Appeal held that collectively appearing at video and photo shoots amounted to a representation by conduct that none of the band were intending to leave and nor were any of the band aware that a member was about to leave.

3. *The misrepresentation must be made before or at the time of the contract*

- A statement made after the formation of a contract cannot amount to a misrepresentation. The formation of the contract was not affected by the statement and neither was a party induced to enter the contract as a result of the statement.

Case	
***Roscorla v Thomas* (1842)**	The seller of a horse stated that the horse was, 'sound and free from vice'. Although the opposite was true, because the promise was made **after** the sale of the horse there was no action for misrepresentation.

4. *The statement must be made by one (the representor) to another (the representee) either directly or indirectly and where both become parties to the contract*

- The representation must have been made by the party (or his agent) against whom relief is required.

5. *The statement must have been material to the decision to enter the contract.*

- The courts have devised an objective test to decide whether a statement alleged to be a misrepresentation was material or significant in the decision to enter a contract.
- If a **reasonable person's** judgement would have been influenced by the statement to enter the contract then the statement is 'material'.

Case:	
***JEB Fasteners Ltd v Marks Bloom & Co.* (1983)**	The claimants launched a takeover of a company with the intention of acquiring the services of two of the current directors and inspected the company's accounts. The accountants had been negligent in preparing them. The action for misrepresentation failed because the purpose of the takeover was to acquire the services of the two directors. The negligently prepared accounts did not act as an inducement and were not materially relevant.

- In contrast it might not matter that a statement isn't normally regarded as an inducement where in fact the claimant was subjectively induced.

Case:	
***Museprime Properties Ltd v Adhill Properties Ltd* (1990)**	Facts: There was an auction sale for three properties. Representations were made during the course of the auction that the rent reviews had not been fixed and it was still possible to negotiate higher rates. This was completely false and new rents had already been fixed. The claimants brought an action for the contract to be revoked on the grounds of misrepresentation. Held: The court rejected the defendant's argument that no reasonable purchaser would have relied on the statements. The court upheld the claimant's claim on the basis that it was enough for the purchaser to show it was material to **their** decision to purchase the properties. The objective test was just a mechanism to help determine the evidence that a claimant needs to convince the court that the statement was material to their decision to enter the contract.

Workpoint

What is the general rule in respect of silence as a misrepresentation of fact?

What is the authority for the general rule?

What are the exceptions to the rule?

- If a party is unaware of a misrepresentation they cannot have been induced by it.
- If a party is already aware that the representation is false then equally there is no inducement. Entering the contract regardless means there will be no misrepresentation.
- As well as being material, the representation must have been relied on. No misrepresentation will occur where there has been no reliance on the statement.

Case	
***Attwood v Small* (1838)**	A mine was purchased and several false representations were made by the vendor regarding the capacity of the mine. The purchasers commissioned their own survey of the mine which supported the representations made by the vendor. An action for misrepresentation was unsuccessful because the purchasers had relied on their own engineer's report and not the representations of the vendor.
***Redgrave v Hurd* (1881)**	A claimant was able to have a contract rescinded on the grounds of misrepresentation despite having had the opportunity to verify the truth of a statement and choosing not to. The statements were relied on and therefore induced the contract. Declining to verify a statement is not a bar to misrepresentation. However if the declining of the invitation is seen as unreasonable then a court may reduce any damages paid on the basis of contributory negligence.

- A claim for misrepresentation will not fail because there were other inducements relied upon as well as the misrepresentation when the contract was entered into (*Edgington v Fitzmaurice* (1885)).
- The diagram below shows how a misrepresentation may arise.

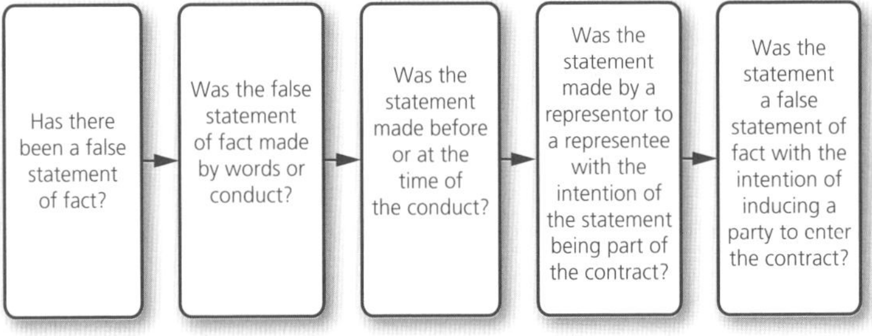

- All of the above are requirements for an actionable misrepresentation. However there will not be an action for misrepresentation should the answer to any of the questions be 'no'.

Workpoint

Is it possible for a misrepresentation to occur that did not induce a party to contract?

What is the general rule on silence amounting to a misrepresentation? What are the exceptions to the rule?

5.3 Misrepresentation, but which one?

- Distinguishing between the various types of misrepresentation is important both in terms of what needs to be proved and what remedies are available.
- Traditionally **fraudulent** and **innocent** misrepresentations were only recognised at common law. During the 1960s there were developments in the law with **negligent** misrepresentation being recognised at common law (*Hedley Byrne & Co. Ltd v Heller & Partners Ltd* (1964)) and in statute (Misrepresentation Act 1967 s 2(1)).

5.3.1 Fraudulent misrepresentation

- Fraudulent misrepresentation, an action in the tort of deceit, was defined by Lord Herschell in the House of Lords in *Derry v Peek* (1889) as a false statement that is:

*'made **knowingly** or **without belief in its truth** or **recklessly careless whether it be true or false**'.*

- The statement may be a deliberate lie.

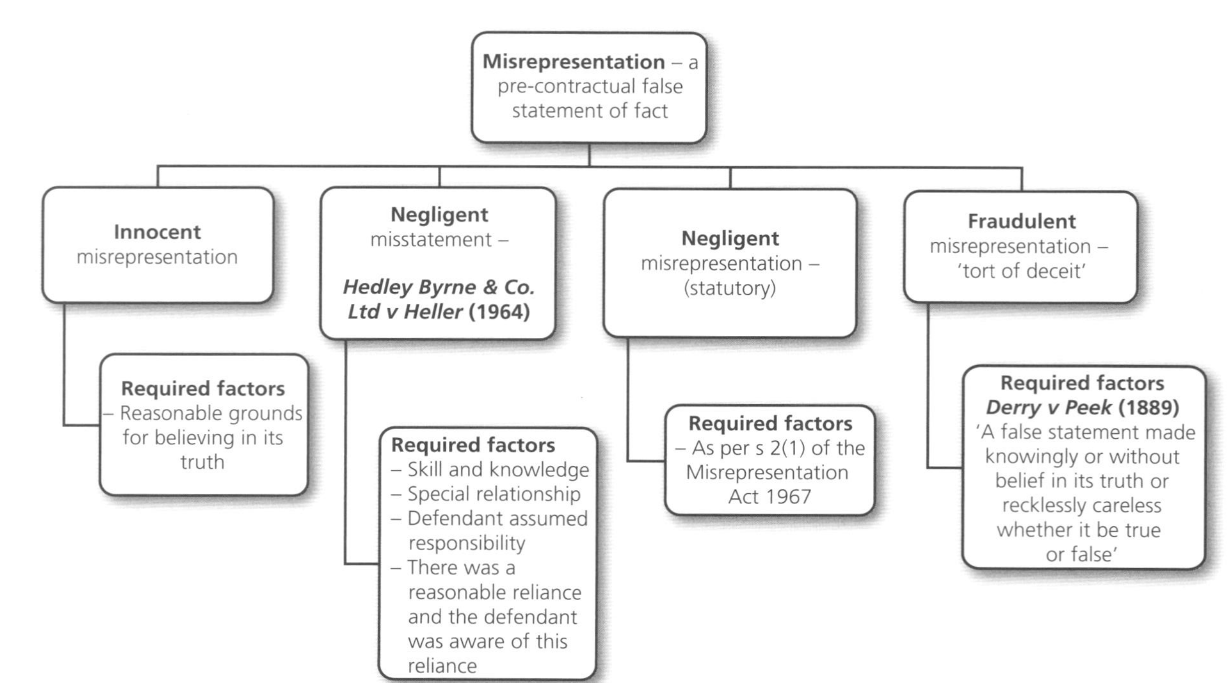
Misrepresentation – a pre-contractual false statement of fact
Innocent misrepresentation
Required factors – Reasonable grounds for believing in its truth
Negligent misstatement – Hedley Byrne & Co. Ltd v Heller (1964)
Required factors – Skill and knowledge – Special relationship – Defendant assumed responsibility – There was a reasonable reliance and the defendant was aware of this reliance
Negligent misrepresentation – (statutory)
Required factors – As per s 2(1) of the Misrepresentation Act 1967
Fraudulent misrepresentation – 'tort of deceit'
Required factors Derry v Peek (1889) 'A false statement made knowingly or without belief in its truth or recklessly careless whether it be true or false'

- If the maker of the statement believed the statement to be true they cannot be liable for fraud.
- Being reckless or careless is not dishonesty in its own right. The court must find dishonesty in that the party could not have rationally believed their statement to be true.
- A reckless or careless statement that the maker genuinely believed to be true will not constitute fraudulent misrepresentation.

Case	
***Thomas Witter Ltd v TBP Industries Ltd* (1996)**	The claimants alleged that the defendants acted recklessly and thus fraudulently in failing to state that they had changed their accounting policy. The court held that the defendants had not acted fraudulently since they believed their statements to be true.

5.3.2 Negligent misrepresentation

Misrepresentation may take two forms:

1. *Common law negligent misstatement*
   - Before *Hedley Byrne & Co. Ltd v Heller & Partners Ltd* (1964) the general consensus was that all misrepresentations were innocent if they were not fraudulent misrepresentations.

Case:	
***Hedley Byrne & Co. Ltd v Heller & Partners Ltd* (1964)**	The House of Lords permitted the common law tort of negligence to cover negligent misstatements causing financial loss. The claimants were asked to provide £100,000 worth of advertising on credit by a particular company ('Easipower'). Easipower's bankers were asked for a reference about the financial situation and creditworthiness of Easipower. The bank knew why the reference was needed and responded with a reference declaring Easipower to be creditworthy and on a sound financial footing. The defendants enclosed with the credit reference a disclaimer stating their reply was 'without responsibility'. Not long after, Easipower went into liquidation and the claimants brought an action for negligent misstatement. The action failed because of the disclaimer given by the bank.

	There was a duty of care owed by the defendants which was negated by the disclaimer. Had there been no disclaimer, the defendants would have owed a duty of care based on the **special relationship** between the parties. The special relationship arises where a party claims a particular skill and it is expected that another will rely on that skill (*Esso Petroleum Co. Ltd v Mardon* (1976)).

- *Caparo Industries Plc v Dickman* (1990) introduced a further requirement of **'proximity'** between the parties thus making the establishment of a duty of care more stringent.
- An action for negligent misrepresentation at common law is therefore based on the tortious action of negligent misstatement pursuant to the *Hedley Byrne* principles. The following must exist:
  - a duty of care
  - sufficient proximity between the parties
  - the party not succeeding in exercising reasonable care and skill when giving advice.

Research Point

Explain the legal principles in the following cases:

1) *Hedley Byrne & Co. Ltd v Heller & Partners Ltd* (1964)

2) *Bisset v Wilkinson* (1927)

3) *Derry v Peek* (1889)

2. *Negligent misrepresentation under the Misrepresentation Act 1967 s 2(1)*

'Where a person has entered into a contract after a misrepresentation has been made to him by another party thereto and as a result thereof has suffered loss, then, if the person making the misrepresentation would be liable in damages in respect thereof had the misrepresentation been made fraudulently, that person shall be so liable notwithstanding that the misrepresentation was not made fraudulently, unless he proves that he had reasonable grounds to believe and did believe up to the time the contract was made that the facts represented were true.'

As a result of the act a party, despite not being able to prove the criteria for fraud or a special relationship (the *Hedley Byrne* principle), may still bring an action for misrepresentation.

Key differences between s 2(1) of the Misrepresentation Act 1967 and negligent misstatement at common law
• There is an assumption in s 2(1) of the Act that the statement made was done so without reasonable grounds for believing in its truth. This is the opposite to *Derry v Peek* where the claimant was required to prove fraud.
• S 2(1) does not require proof of a duty of care or a special relationship.
• S 2(1) only applies where the claimant has 'entered into a contract'.
• Under a negligent misstatement claim an action may be brought by a third party.
• Under the common law a statement may well be an opinion and as such not will not require the proof that a misrepresentation had been made.

Case	
***Howard Marine Dredging Co. Ltd v A Ogden & Sons (Excavating) Ltd* (1978)**	Where a party disproves negligence and they demonstrate reasonable grounds for belief in the truth of the statement, they will avoid liability under s 2(1) of the Misrepresentation Act 1967.

5.3.3 Innocent misrepresentation

Owing to the Misrepresentation Act 1967 s 2(1) and the *Hedley Byrne* principle a person must make a statement with an honest belief in its truth for a misrepresentation to be made innocently. As an alternative to rescission, under s 2(2) a court may award damages.

Research Point

Under s 2(1) of the Misrepresentation Act 1967 upon whom does the burden of proof rely?

What remedy is available under s 2(2) of the Misrepresentation Act 1967 should s 2(1) not be available?

5.4 Remedies for misrepresentation

Should an action for misrepresentation be successful there will be two remedies available, **damages** and **rescission**.

- The general rule is that a contract will be rendered voidable (but not void) until the point that the representee decides to have the contract set aside or affirmed. Should the party wish to affirm the contract they act in a manner that would be considered by a reasonable person to be consistent with wishing the contract to be proceeded with.

Definition

Affirm: 'To carry on with'. Where A seeks to have a contract with B affirmed, A seeks to carry on the contract with B.

- A representee may also end the performance of their obligations under a contract and allow an action to be brought against them for breach of contract, thus invoking the defence of misrepresentation.
- Rescission is available for all misrepresentations. It sets aside the contract and the parties are placed in the position they were before the contract was made. Rescission is achieved either by notifying the party or acting in a manner which would suggest that rescission is the intention of the representee.

Research Point

What were the facts of *Car and Universal Finance Ltd v Caldwell* (1965)?

Do you agree with the decision of the Court of Appeal?

5.4.1 Bars to rescission

- There are four circumstances in which a party may not be entitled to the remedy of rescission.

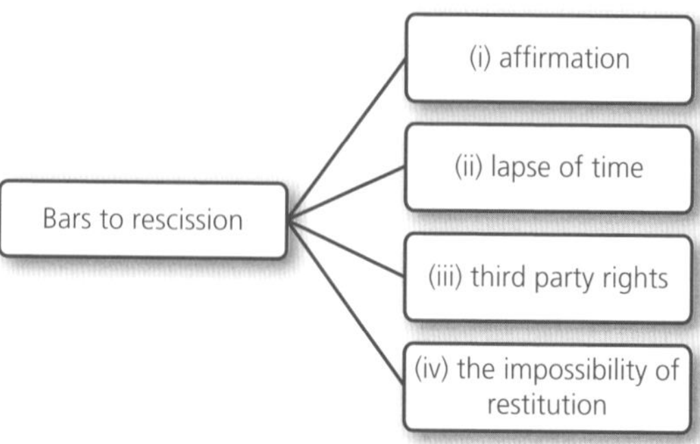

5.4.1.1 Affirmation

- If a party affirms the contract they waive the right to have it rescinded and may not retract the affirmation. Should a party discover a misrepresentation and fail to act, a court may decide that affirmation has occurred.

Case:	
***Long v Lloyd* (1958)**	The claimants bought a lorry from the defendants after being assured it was in good condition. When problems with the lorry were pointed out to the defendant it was agreed that the defendant and claimant would each pay half to have the lorry repaired. When the lorry again had problems the claimant brought an action for innocent misrepresentation and the rescission of the contract. The defendants' representations whilst false were honestly made. The court held that having accepted an offer for part payment towards the initial repairs the claimants had forgone their right to rescission.

5.4.1.2 Lapse of time

- Lapse of time is evidence of affirmation and time begins from the point the misrepresentation is discovered. This is the case for fraudulent misrepresentation.
- For innocent and negligent misrepresentation, the time begins from the date of the contract. The rescission must take place within a reasonable time.

Case:	
***Leaf v International Galleries* (1950)**	The claimant had bought a painting and five years later, having realised it was not painted by Constable, unsuccessfully sought rescission. Despite there being no evidence of affirmation the court held a time lapse of five years barred the claimant from rescission.

5.4.1.3 Third party rights

- Where a third party has acquired rights in the subject matter of the contract in good faith and for a value there will be no right of rescission; for example, should Tammy obtain a ring from Vern by misrepresentation and Gemma then buys the ring from Tammy in good faith, Vern would not have the remedy of rescission having learnt of the misrepresentation. Gemma now has rights.

5.4.1.4 'Restitutio in integrum' – rescission is impossible

Definition

Restitutio in integrum: Restoration to the original position.

- For one reason or another it may not be possible to place the parties in the position they were pre-contractually. The good may have been destroyed, perished or had its value diminished as in *Armstrong v Jackson* (1917).

Case	
***Vigers v Pike* (1842)**	Due to large scale extraction from a mine its restitution was not achievable. The remedy is still available if extensive restoration is achievable.

5.4.2 Damages

- It is possible that rescission will not be a sufficient remedy where a significant loss has occurred.

Type of misrepresentation	Explanation of damages available	Case/s
Fraudulent misrepresentation	Follows the tort measure of assessing damages. The claimant will be placed in the position they would have been had the tort not occurred.	*Doyle v Olby (Ironmongers) Ltd* (1969) affirms this and the principle that the claimant may recover '**all consequential losses**' as a result of fraudulent misrepresentation.
Negligent misrepresentation	(i) *At common law:* based on the negligent misstatement principle laid down in *Hedley Byrne v Heller*. Awarded under tortious principle of remoteness and what was '**reasonably foreseeable**'.	In *Overseas Tankship (UK) Ltd v Morts Dock & Engineering Co. (The Wagon Mound)* (1961) it was confirmed in applying the test of remoteness that the claimant of negligent misstatement will only be able to

Type of misrepresentation	Explanation of damages available	Case/s
		recover damages that were 'reasonably foreseeable' in the eyes of the defendant as a result of the misrepresentation.
	(ii) *Action brought under s 2(1)*: damages are calculated according to the tort measure.	This has not always been the case, with *Watts v Spence* (1976) applying a contractual measure. It was however confirmed that the tortious approach was the correct one in *Andre et Cie SA v Ets Michel Blanc et Fils* (1977) and then in *Sharneyford Supplies Ltd v Edge* (1985).
Innocent misrepresentation	There is no right to damages and they are not usually recoverable unless the court exercises discretion under s 2(2). S 2(3) suggests the measure of damages should not be the same as s 2(1)	*William Sindall plc v Cambridgeshire County Council* (1994) suggests the difference in value of what the claimant received and that which he thought he would receive as a measure.

5.5 Exclusion of liability for misrepresentation

- It is possible for a contract to contain a clause that aims to exclude or limit any liability for misrepresentation. S 3 of the Misrepresentation Act 1967 as amended by s 8 of the Unfair Contract Terms Act 1977 states:

> *'If a contract contains a term which would exclude or restrict:*
>
> *(a) any liability to which a party to a contract may be subject by reason of any misrepresentation made by him before the contract was made; or*
>
> *(b) any remedy available to another party to the contract by reason of such a misrepresentation, that term shall be of no effect except in so far as it satisfies the requirement of reasonableness as stated in s 11(1) of the Unfair Contract Terms Act 1977; and it is for those claiming that the term satisfies that requirement to show that it does.'*

- The exclusion clause excluding misrepresentation is subject to and must pass the same test of reasonableness as all other exemption clauses to which s 11(1) of the Unfair Contract Terms Act 1977 applies. S 11 states:

> *'... the term shall have been a fair and reasonable one to be included having regard to the circumstances which were, or ought reasonably to have been, known to or in the contemplation of the parties when the contract was made.'*

- A strict approach is required.

Case:	
***Thomas Whitter Ltd v TBP Industries Ltd* (1996)**	The clause stated 'Liability for any pre-contractual misrepresentation will be excluded.'
***Walker v Boyle* (1982)**	Where answers were given to enquiries made regarding the sale of a property, there was a clause excluding liability for any errors, misstatements or omissions. An innocent but mistaken answer given by the seller said there were no boundary disputes. The exclusion clause was held to be unreasonable by the court.

Workpoint

When may rescission not be available and under what circumstances may it not be an adequate remedy?

Research Point

Should the bars to rescission be removed?

5.6 Summary

- Having distinguished between a term and a representation, a misrepresentation is a false statement of fact made by a representor to a representee without the intention of it becoming an element of the contract.
- The types of misrepresentation are fraudulent, negligent misstatement at common law, negligent (Misrepresentation Act 1967) and innocent.
- A party may avoid their obligations under the contract and will have the right to damages or rescission.
- Only a false statement of fact will enable an action for misrepresentation. Unless made fraudulently, a statement of future intention or opinion will not be actionable.

Checkpoint – misrepresentation

Item on checklist:	**Done!**
I can define misrepresentation	
I can explain the requirements for misrepresentation	
I can define the different forms of misrepresentation	
I can define the rule relating to silence as a misrepresentation of fact	
I can state and support with case law the exceptions to the rule relating to silence as a misrepresentation of fact	
I can explain the remedies available for misrepresentation	
I can explain the bars to rescission	
I can state how and why an exclusion of liability clause for misrepresentation may or may not be upheld by a court	

Potential exam questions

Peter and Tim have been best friends for 12 years. Peter is selling his yacht 'The Peacock' in Monaco for £70,000. He tells Tim it is only two years old and has recently been serviced with a brand new gear exchange system fitted and starter motor. In fact it is five years old; the previous gear exchange system had been fixed with second hand parts and the starter motor has repeatedly failed to start the engine. During the course of negotiations Peter provides Tim with the ownership documents which detail the service and maintenance history since the yacht was first made. If Tim had looked at the documents he would have seen the true age of the yacht.

On Tim's next trip to Monaco three months later he meets up with his old friend Peter and agrees to buy the yacht for £70,000. Within minutes of leaving port the gears fail and Tim returns the yacht to Peter and accepts his offer to fix the yacht. On a family holiday four months later when Tim attempts to start the yacht the starter motor ignites. The fire causes serious external and internal damage.

Advise Tim.

How would your advice be different if Tim, not bothered about the age or maintenance of the yacht, instead bought it for its distinct yellow, white and blue colours?

Chapter 6
Mistake

6.1 Introduction

- An actionable misrepresentation will render a contract *voidable*. However, a mistake by one of the parties to the contract will render a contract *void*.
- For the validity of the contract to be at risk the mistake must be an operative one. Should the mistake not be an operative one then it may be possible that equity intervenes and the contract becomes voidable.
- Whilst there are many 'doctrines' in contract law there is not a doctrine of mistake. The effect of a mistake at common law is to render the contract void, *ab initio*, that is from the beginning, with the common law refusing to recognise the existence of the contract. As a result no obligations can occur and no title to the goods can pass.
- Where a third party has acquired rights in the subject matter a court will not allow rescission where a misrepresentation has occurred. However, where a contract is void because of a mistake no title will have passed from buyer to seller or any possible third party. The original buyer or the third party will have acquired no rights and the subject matter would have to be returned to the seller. This approach is affirmed by the latin maxim *nemo dat quod non habet*.

Definition

Nemo dat quod non habet: No one may transfer ownership of something they do not own.

- Mistake, like misrepresentation, is a vitiating factor and invalidates consent. The lack of indisputable consent means an agreement between parties is invalid despite the contract containing offer, acceptance, intention and consideration.

Case	
***Bell v Lever Bros Ltd* (1932)**	**Lord Atkin**: 'If mistake operates at all, it operates so as to negate or in some cases nullify consent.'

There are three categories of mistake:

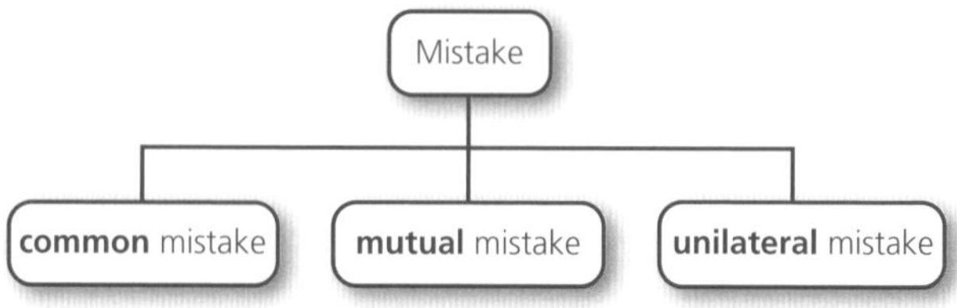

- **Common mistake** – where **both** parties are mistaken about the subject matter, its quality or ownership. There are three different categories of common mistake:

  1. *res extincta*
  2. *res sua*
  3. mistake as to the quality of the subject matter.

- **Mutual mistake** – The parties are at cross-purposes and should this be the case the contract is void. The parties do not realise there is a misunderstanding between them. A mutual mistake may arise as a result of:

  1. the terms of the contract
  2. the subject matter of the contract.

- **Unilateral mistake** – one of the parties is entering into the contract under a mistake. The other party is not only aware of the mistake but is seeking to take advantage of it. There is usually a mistake in:

  1. the terms of the contract
  2. identity of the contracting parties
  3. *non est factum* (documents signed by mistake).

Definition

Res extincta: A mistake as to the subject matter's **existence.**

Res sua: A mistake as to the subject matter's **ownership.**

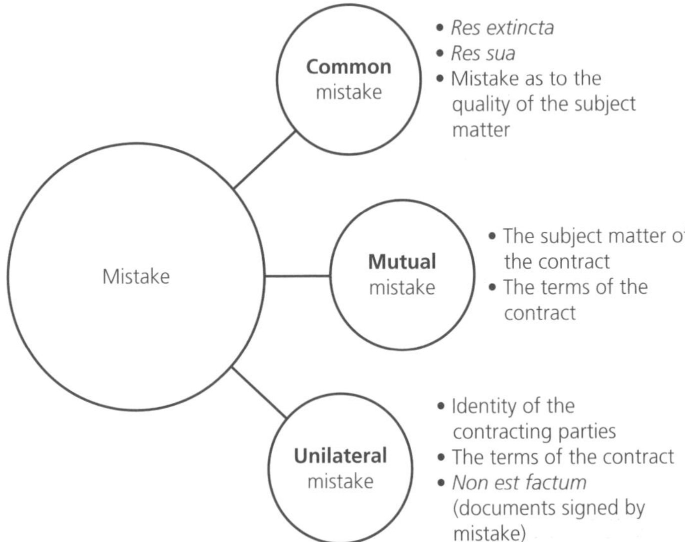

6.2 Common mistake

6.2.1 Common mistake – *res extincta*

- Here both parties have made a mistake as to the existence of the subject matter. Should this be the case performance will be impossible and the contract is void.
- In *Galloway v Galloway* (1914) a man and woman assumed they were married but in fact they were not and as a result a separation deed was void.
- The principle of the subject matter no longer existing at the time of entering into the contract, thus rendering a contract void for common mistake, is given a statutory footing by the Sale of Goods Act 1979 s 6:

  'Where there is a contract for the sale of specific goods, and the goods without the knowledge of the seller have perished at the time when the contract is made, the contract is void.'

Case:	
***Couturier v Hastie* (1856)**	This case illustrates that where the subject matter does not exist when the contract is formed then the contract cannot exist either. The principle of *res extincta* renders such a contract void. In this case a contract had been agreed for the sale of Indian corn

	in transit. Both parties believed the corn existed at the time of the contract. However, a few days before the contract was made and without either party knowing, the cargo began to ferment and before it could ferment further the captain of the ship sold it. This was accepted as normal custom. The buyer claimed the contract was void as before entering into the contract the corn had ceased to exist. The House of Lords, without mentioning mistake, held that the buyer was not obliged to pay for the cargo and the seller was not obliged to deliver the goods since the contract contemplated the existence of goods that in reality didn't exist. Lord Cranworth: *'looking to the contract itself alone, it appears to me clearly that what the parties contemplated, those who bought and those who sold, was that there was an existing something to be sold and bought … The contract plainly imports that there was something which was to be sold at the time of the contract, and something to be purchased. No such thing existing … there must be judgement … for the defendants.'*

Case	
***McRae v Commonwealth Disposals Commission* (1950)**	The court concluded that where the subject matter was non-existent but a party had 'warranted' its existence the contract would be valid and the party could be held liable for breach of contract and for the payment of damages.

Workpoint

How will a court decide a claim of *res extincta* where:

1) the subject matter existed but was destroyed before the formation of the contract? and
2) where the subject matter never existed at all?

6.2.2 Common mistake – *res sua*

- Should a buyer agree to purchase something from a seller which they already have title to, then providing neither party was aware of the true title, the contract will be void for mistake at common law. This is known as *res sua*.
- It is very rare, but not impossible that one may purchase something one already owns. In *Cooper v Phibbs* (1867) a nephew mistakenly bought a lease for property he already owned from his deceased uncle's daughter.

Workpoint

What is the essential difference between *res extincta* and *res sua?*

6.2.3 Common mistake – mistake as to the quality of the subject matter

- The issue of **quality** is complex. The question that arises is whether or not a contract is void where the parties to the contract do not believe the subject matter has the anticipated quality.
- The starting point and leading case is *Bell v Lever Bros* (1932).

Case	
***Bell v Lever Bros* (1932)**	Lever Brothers entered into an agreement with Bell (an employee) to leave the company in exchange for £30,000 compensation. It was later apparent that the company would have been able to terminate Bell's contract without payment as a result of Bell's involvement in conflicting contracts. The company sought the recovery of £30,000 believing that Bell had been paid the money mistakenly. The court held there was no operative mistake and there had been a valid contract. The mistake was purely down to the quality of contract of service. The mistake was not **fundamental** to the making of the agreed settlement. Lord Atkin expressed his test: *'Mistake as to the quality of the thing contracted for raises more difficult questions. In such a case a mistake will not affect assent unless it is the mistake of both parties, and is as to the existence of some quality which makes the thing without the quality essentially different from the thing as it was believed to be.'*

	This did not include, for example, where parties thought a painting to be genuine when it was actually a fake: *'A buys a picture from B: both A and B believe it to be the work of an old master, and a high price is paid. It turns out to be a modern copy. A has no remedy in the absence of representation or warranty.'*

Workpoint

What are the facts and decision of *Green Peace Shipping Ltd v Tsavliris Salvage (International) Ltd* (2002)?

Does the case of *Associated Japanese Bank (International) Ltd v Credit du Nord SA* (1988) affirm the decision given in *Green Peace Shipping*?

- Further evidence that a contract will not be void for mistake where the mistake is one relating to the quality of the subject matter can be found in *Leaf v International Galleries* (1950). The claimant bought a painting believing it to be a Constable. He discovered some time in the future that this was not the case and brought an action for misrepresentation. The court, *obiter*, held approving *Bell v Lever Brothers* that the contract would not have been void for mistake. Denning LJ stated:

'There was a mistake about the quality of the subject matter, because both parties believed the picture to be a Constable; and that mistake was in one sense essential or fundamental. But such a mistake does not avoid the contract: there was no mistake at all about the subject matter of the sale. It was a specific picture, 'Salisbury Cathedral'. The parties were agreed in the same terms on the subject matter, and that is sufficient to make a contract.'

Common mistake	Explanation	The contract
Res extincta	The subject matter does not exist at the time of the contract	*VOID*

Common mistake	Explanation	The contract
Res sua	Neither the buyer nor seller is aware that the buyer already has title to the subject matter when the parties contract.	*VOID*
Mistake as to the **quality** of the subject matter	If the only mistake is as to quality the court will not seek to protect a party merely because they got a bad bargain.	*CONTRACT CONTINUES*

6.3 Mutual mistake

Definition

Mutual mistake: Both parties have made different mistakes and are at cross-purposes.

- Both parties are at cross-purposes and have a mistaken belief over the other's intentions. The mistake is a fundamental factual mistake that goes to the very heart of the contract with, for example, Les offering a car with Julie thinking she is getting a space ship.
- In the above example offer and acceptance do not coincide and as such the contract is void. There is a lack of *consensus ad idem*.

Definition

Consensus ad idem: A 'meeting of minds' where both parties have the same understanding of the terms of a contract.

Research Point

In what ways are common and mutual mistake different?

6.3.1 Mutual mistake – terms of the contract

- The test is an objective one. The courts will endeavour to find agreement between the parties. If they can do this the contract will be allowed to run its course on what the court believes to be the true intention of the parties.

- Should the courts be unable to find an agreement and performance of the contract proves impossible, the contract will be void for mistake.

Case:	
***Raffles v Wichelhaus* (1864)**	Two ships named *Peerless*, both loaded with cotton, were departing Bombay; one in October and one in December. The defendant thought the contract for the sale of cotton referred to the cotton aboard the October ship whilst the claimant assumed the contract was for the cotton aboard the December ship. No common consensus could be found; the contract could not be performed and as such the court held the contract to be void for mistake.

6.3.2 Mutual mistake – subject matter of the contract

- Should there be any uncertainty or misunderstanding about the subject matter of the contract this will also render the contract void.

Case:	
***Scriven Bros & Co. v Hindley & Co.* (1913)**	At auction a bidder mistakenly bought a quantity of tow thinking it was hemp (which had a greater value). This was because the auctioneers wrongly labelled the cargo when it arrived. Once he realised he had not purchased hemp he refused to pay for the tow. The court decided there was no chance of the matter being resolved to the satisfaction of both parties and no third party would have been capable of concluding whether the contract was for hemp or tow. Subsequently the contract was declared void.

- Where one party is mistaken as to the quality of the goods and the contract may still be performed the contract will not be void: *Smith v Hughes* (1871).

Research Point

Why were the cases of *Raffles v Wichelhaus* (1864) and *Smith v Hughes* (1871) decided differently?

6.4 Unilateral mistake

Definition

Unilateral mistake: One party to the contract is mistaken and the other party is aware, or the circumstances suggest they should be aware, of the mistake.

- The test is now one of subjectivity and not objectivity. Again the contract will be void providing the mistake is 'fundamental'.
- There are also three further requirements for the mistake to be operative:
  1. The mistake must relate *to a term of the contract* (*Sybron Corporation v Rochem* (1984)).
  2. The non-mistaken party must be aware of, or should have reasonably known of, the mistake (*Wood v Scarth* (1858)).
  3. The mistaken party must not be at fault.

6.4.1 Unilateral mistake – terms of the contract

When expressing their intentions, if a party makes a mistake and the other party is aware, or the circumstances suggest they should have been aware, then the mistake will be operative and the contract declared void.

Case:	
***Hartog v Colin & Shields* (1939)**	The contract involved the sale by the defendants of 30,000 Argentine hare skins at 30d **per skin**. The claimants brought an action to hold the defendants to a written offer when they later mistakenly sold the offered the skins for 10d **per lb** (around a third of the originally discussed price). The contract was declared void with the court saying that the claimant must have known about the mistake and the material mistake concerned a term of the contract (price per pound as opposed to price per piece).

6.4.1.1 Unilateral mistake – identity

- This area of mistake can be complicated. However the example below is one which we will consider a familiar situation:

> **Common example** – party A makes off with property belonging to party B after making false statements as to their identity. This is then the mistake of B. The property is then transferred to C (a third party) by party A.

- Considering the example above party B could claim fraudulent misrepresentation. Should this be successful the contract will be rendered *voidable*.
- If the contract wasn't voided before the property was transferred to C then C will have acquired title to the property.
- We know, however, that a successful claim for mistake will render the contract *void*. The effect of which is that the contract never existed. As a result no title could have passed from B to A to C (the third party).
- The consequence of this is that C will have to return the property to B despite the property being obtained in good faith.
- If it is possible and A has not disappeared, then C may sue for breach of contract for breach of an implied term under the Sale of Goods Act 1979 s 12.

Voidable contract:

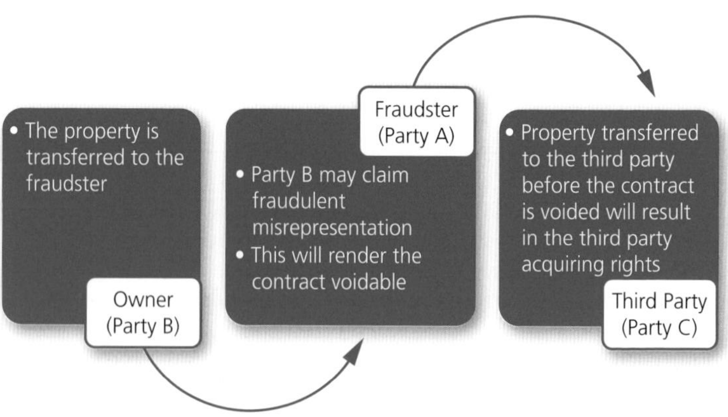

Void contract:

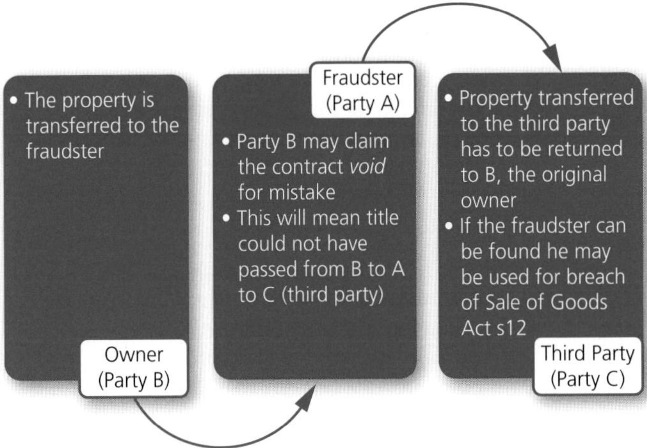

- In the case of mistaken identity, the contract will only be void where it can be shown that:

1. **The mistake must have been material and of fundamental importance to the contract. The mistake must be operative and the party must have entered into the contract as a result of it.**

Case:	
***Cundy v Lindsay* (1878)**	Facts: Lindsay received an order for handkerchiefs from a fraudster called Alfred Blenkarn. He signed his name so as to resemble that of W Blenkiron & Co., a highly respectable company on the same street. He gave his address as 37 Wood Street. Alfred Blenkarn took receipt, without paying for the goods at number 37 Wood Street and then sold some to Cundy. Held: The House of Lords held the contract void for mistake. By showing that whoever was trading from 37 Wood Street was fundamental to the formation of the contract and thus operable.

2. **They must prove that they intended to contract with a party other than the one that they actually contracted with. A false name will not necessarily mean that the mistake is an operative one.**

Case:	
***King's Norton Metal Co. Ltd v Edridge, Merret & Co. Ltd* (1897)**	Facts: The claimant received an order from 'Hallam & Co., Soho Hackle Pin & Wire Works' called 'Hallam & Co.', on headed paper and the company purported to be of sound financial footing with an international reputation. In fact it was a fraudster. Relying on the alleged reputation, the claimants sent the goods which the fraudster then failed to pay for and in turn sold them to the defendants. Held: Here the Court of Appeal held there was no operative mistake. The mistake was with respect of the creditworthiness of the defendants. The claimants failed to prove that they had intended to contract with someone else. Smith L.J: *'The question was, with whom, upon this evidence, which was all one way, did the plaintiffs contract to sell the goods?* ***Clearly with the writer of the letters****. If it could have been shown that there was a separate entity called Hallam and Co. and another entity called Wallis then the case might have come within the decision in* Cundy v Lindsay. *In his opinion there was a contract by the plaintiffs with the person who wrote the letters, by which the property passed to him. There was only one entity, trading under an alias, and there was a contract by which the property passed to him.'*

3. **The mistaken party must show that the other party was aware of the mistake before or at the time of the contact in order to prove the mistake is material.**

Case:	
***Boulton v Jones* (1857)**	An order placed by the defendant addressed to Brocklehurst was sent to Boulton. Boulton therefore knew that it wasn't meant for him. A party accepting an offer knowing it to be for someone else assumes the possibility that the mistake may be material.

Workpoint

Andy is the owner of a signed 1972 FA Cup winning shirt. Tom tells Andy he is from the Football Association and is looking to purchase items for the walls and corridors of the new Football Association HQ being built in Leeds. Accepting a cheque from Tom, Andy hands over the shirt. Andy has now discovered the man was not from the Football Association; the cheque has bounced; the Football Association has no intention of moving from its current HQ; and Tom, whose real name is Darren, has sold the shirt to Leigh via an online auction site.

Advise Andy and Leigh.

6.4.1.2 Unilateral mistake – mistaken identity and contracts made 'face-to-face'

- Where a contract is made face-to-face the contract is considered to have been formed with the actual person present.
- It doesn't matter what identity they have assumed.
- The mistake will be in respect of a person's attributes, such as credit-worthiness.
- The mistake is not operative or material and as such, the contract **cannot** be declared void.
- The same can also be said should the contract be made through an intermediary (*Shogun Finance Ltd v Hudson* (2004)).

Case:	
***Phillips v Brooks Ltd* (1919)**	A man walked into a jewellers' shop and selected a ring worth £450. He claimed to be Sir George Bullough of St James's Square. The claimant checked the address of the man and then accepted a cheque as payment for the ring. The cheque bounced and the man was not Sir George Bullough but a fraudster. The fraudster sold the ring to a third party, whilst the vlaimant tried to sue for its recovery. Horridge J held there was no operative mistake regarding identity and the third party had good title to the ring. The claimant was more concerned with the individual's ability to pay than their identity which was not deemed to have been of fundamental importance.

Research Point

What are the facts of *Lewis v Averay* (1972) and *Ingram v Little* (1960)?

Why was the case of *Ingram v Little* (1960) decided differently to that of *Phillips v Brooks* (1919) and *Lewis v Averay* (1972)?

In *Lewis v Averay* (1972) did Magaw LJ agree support or dismiss the test given in *Ingram v Little* (1960)?

- *Lewis v Averay* in the Court of Appeal followed *Phillips v Brooks* in stating that although the contract was voidable for fraudulent misrepresentation, it was not void for mistake. The claimant intended to deal with the person in front of them, regardless of their identity.

Lord Denning MR stated:

'When a dealing is had between a seller like the claimant and a person who is actually there present before him, then the presumption in law is that there is a contract, even though there is a fraudulent impersonation by the buyer representing himself as a different man than he is. There is a contract made with the very person there … '.

Reasonable steps should be taken in order to check the identity of the party being contracted with should a party allege the mistake was material to the making of the contract, *Citibank NA v Brown Shipley & Co. Ltd; Midland Bank plc v Brown Shipley & Co. Ltd* (1991).

Case:	
***Shogun Finance Ltd v Hudson* (2004)**	Facts: A fraudster purchased a car on hire-purchase terms using the stolen identity and driving licence of Mr Patel. The claimant finance company received a signed faxed copy of the draft hire-purchase agreement signed by the fraudster in the name of Mr Patel. The claimant company then checked the credit history of the real Mr Patel and agreed a finance package. The fraudster having driven the car away then sold it to the defendant, Hudson.

	Held: The House of Lords decided the current law was correct in respect of mistake as to identity including contracts made *inter praesentes* and *inter absentes*. The House of Lords applied *Cundy v Lindsay* and confirmed that where a contract is made in writing, the parties are, on the face of it, those described in the documentation. As such the contract was between the finance company and Mr Patel. However, because the real Mr Patel had never intended to enter into an agreement with the finance company, the contract was void for mistake as to identity and as such, rather strictly, Hudson was liable for the return of the car. A seller cannot pass on title if he doesn't have it (*nemo dat quod non habet*).

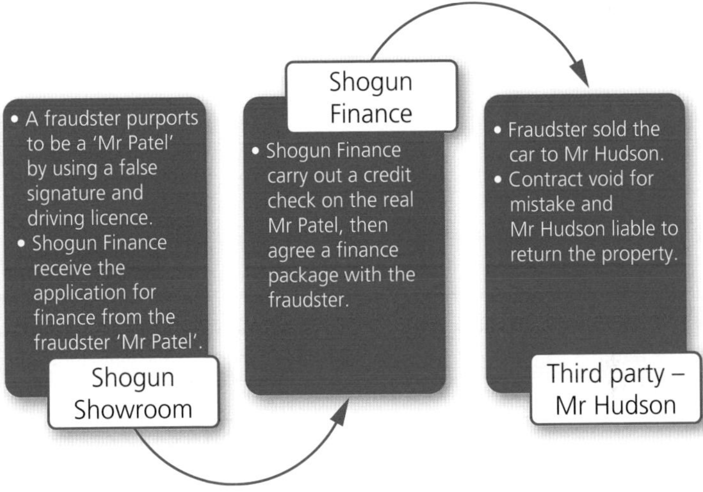

Workpoint

What must an original owner satisfy in order to claim they retain ownership in a case of mistaken identity?

Class of mistake	Key case
Common mistake • *Res estincta* • *Res sua* • Mistake as to quality of subject matter	 • *Couturier v Hastie* • *Cooper v Phibbs* • *Bell v Lever Bros*

Mutual mistake	
• Parties are at cross-purposes	• *Raffles v Wichelhaus* • *Smith v Hughes*
Unilateral mistake	
• Mistake as to terms • Mistaken identity • Mistaken identity (face-to-face)	• *Hartog v Colin & Shields* • *Cundy v Lindsay* • *Lewis v Averay*

6.4.2 *Non est factum* – 'this is not my deed'

Definition

Non est factum: A mistake in respect of a written agreement.

- In limited circumstances a party may claim they have signed a document by mistake. In order to claim this the following must be proved:

1. The contract was vitally different from that which they expected to sign.
2. They must not have been careless in signing the document.

Case:	
***Saunders v Anglia Building Society* (1971)**	Facts: An elderly lady transferred property to her nephew on the provision that she would see out her days in the property. He intended to use the property as security for a loan. The nephew's friend presented a document to the elderly lady which he claimed transferred property to the nephew when in actual fact it transferred property to him. She did not read the document before signing it. Held: The court rejected the *non est factum* claim finding for the building society on the grounds that the document was **not** fundamentally different and she had been careless in not reading it before it was signed.

Research Point

Was *non est factum* pleaded successfully in *Lloyds Bank plc v Waterhouse* (1991)?

6.5 Mistake and the effect of equity

An equitable solution may be found where a mistake is not operative in three ways:

1. rescission
2. rectification
3. refusal to grant a party's claim for specific performance.

1. Rescission → The rescission of a contract will occur where it is unethical or immoral to allow a party to take advantage of a mistake. *Solle v Butcher* (1950)

Research Point

What effect has *Green Peace Shipping Tsavliris* (2002) had on *Solle v Butcher*?

2. Rectification → If there is evidence to suggest the contract does not reflect the true arrangements between the parties then the contract may be 'rectified' accordingly. If a party cannot show that the written agreement is contradictory to the intentions of parties rectification will not be granted.

Craddock Bros Ltd v Hunt (1923)

3. A refusal to grant another's request for specific performance

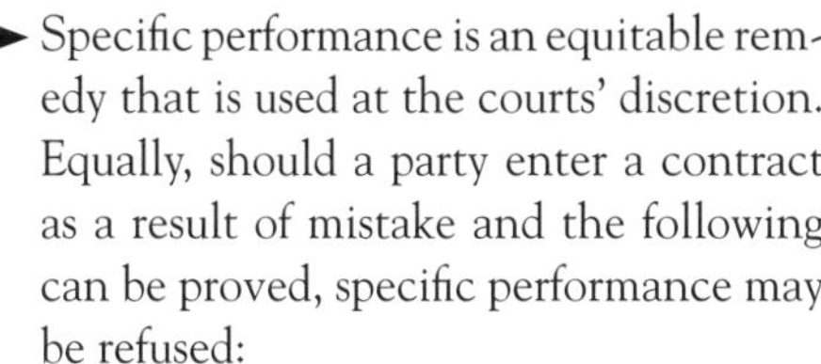

→ Specific performance is an equitable remedy that is used at the courts' discretion. Equally, should a party enter a contract as a result of mistake and the following can be proved, specific performance may be refused:

i. it would be unconscionable to compel a party to continue its obligations under the contract;

ii. the other party, knowing of the mistake, attempted to take advantage of it (*Webster v Cecil* (1861)); or

iii. the other party's misrepresentation caused the mistake.

Checkpoint – mistake

Item on checklist:	**Done!**
I can discuss the similarities and differences between mistake and misrepresentation	
I can define the different classes of mistake	
I can explain the requirements to successfully prove the different types of mistake	
I can define the significance of *Green Peace Shipping Ltd v Tsavliris Salvage (International) Ltd* (2002)	
I can differentiate between situations where the contract might be void and voidable	
I can explain the significance of *Shogun Finance Ltd v Hudson* (2004)	
I can define the presumptions where contracts are concluded at a distance (in writing) and face-to-face	
I can explain the relationship between equity and mistake	

Possible exam question

1) The law relating to mistaken identity has been described by lawyers as fraught with indifference and not helped in the slightest by *Shogun Finance v Hudson* (2004) and the decision of the House of Lords.

   Discuss.

2) Adam owns a life-size Formula 1 helmet and a smaller miniature helmet keyring 'collectors' version. He paid £3,000 for the life-size helmet and £400 for the miniature helmet. They are both thought to have been owned by Lewis Hamilton during

his 2008 World Championship winning season. Such items are becoming increasingly rare to find and as such the value of the items has steadily increased. Adam emails Emily, a work colleague, offering his Formula 1 'prized helmet' (the miniature version) for £500. The next day at work Emily meets Adam at the water cooler and accepts his offer saying, 'I don't know much about Formula 1 but I bet my mum will love it!' Emily in fact wanted the life-size Formula 1 helmet. Adam delivers the smaller miniature helmet when Emily is working overtime that evening. Emily's dad Colin, a Formula 1 fanatic, telephones Emily immediately at work and says that the helmet keyring is in poor condition and only worth approximately £60, and that in any event had it been in good condition it would have only been worth £200. Adam is refusing to take the item back.

Advise Adam and Emily.

Chapter 7
Duress and undue influence

7.1 Introduction

- Should a party exert unreasonable pressure on another the matter would be subject to the common law doctrine of duress and the equitable doctrine of undue influence. A legally binding contract can only arise where the parties have freely consented to be bound by its terms.

Definition

Duress: Where a party is induced to enter a contract by violence or threats of violence.

Undue influence: Where a party is induced to enter a contract by improper and unfair pressure.

- If either a common law action for duress or a claim of undue influence in equity is successful the contract will be **voidable**.

7.2 Duress

- Duress may be divided in three subcategories as illustrated below:

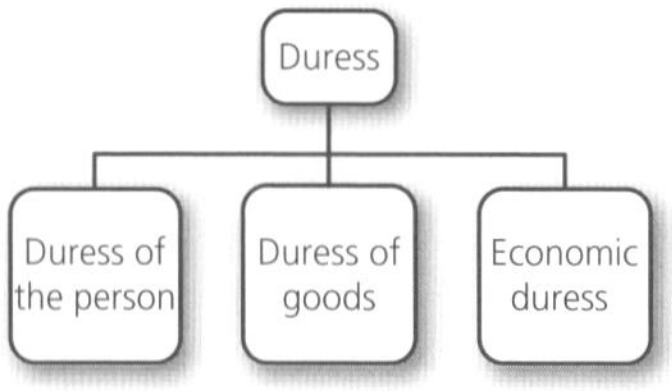

7.2.1 Duress of the person

- For there to be duress there must be actual physical violence or the threat of physical violence, or unlawful constraint, *Cumming v Ince* (1847). The violence must be unlawful, *Biffin v Bignell* (1862).

- 'Duress ... is the threat of harm made to compel a person to do something against his or her will or judgment, esp., a wrongful threat made by one person to compel a manifestation of seeming assent by another person to a transaction without real volition.' *Black's Law Dictionary* (8th edn 2004)

Case:	
***Barton v Armstrong* (1975)**	The Privy Council affirmed that an action for duress will succeed where it can be shown that duress was a factor that induced a party to enter into the contract. It is not necessary to show duress was the only inducement. The burden will shift to the defendant where a threat has been recognised with the defendant being required to prove the threat had nothing to do with the party's decision to contract.

- Threats to carry out a **lawful** action will not amount to duress (*Williams v Bayley* (1886)).

7.2.2 Duress of goods

- A threat against property was not previously considered to be duress (*Skeate v Beale* (1840)). However the courts seem to now recognise the 'duress of goods' and threats posed to property.

Case:	
***Occidental Worldwide Investment Corporation v Skibbs A/S Avanti (The Siboen and The Sibotre)* (1976)**	Kerr J: *'For instance if I should be compelled to sign a ... contract for a nominal but legally sufficient consideration under an imminent threat of having my house burnt down or a valuable picture slashed through without any threat of physical violence to anyone, I do not think the law should uphold the agreement. I think a plea of coercion or compulsion would be available in such cases. The true question is ultimately whether or not the agreement in question is to be regarded as having been concluded voluntarily.'*

Research Point

Is the assertion by Kerr J in *Occidental* supported by Mocatta J in *North Ocean Shipping Co. v Hyundai Construction Co. (The Atlantic Baron)* (1979) or by Lord Scarman in *Pao On v Lau Yiu Long* (1980)?

7.2.3 Economic duress

- The doctrine of economic duress has developed over the last 30 years. It occurs where there may not necessarily have been a threat of violence but there is evidence of intense coercion and unacceptable economic pressure.

Case:	
***The Evia Luck* (1992)**	Lord Goff: *'It is now accepted that economic pressure may be sufficient to amount to duress … provided at least that the economic pressure may be characterised as illegitimate and has constituted a significant cause inducing the claimant to enter into the relevant contract.'*

- A formal doctrine for economic duress was first established in *Occidental* where Kerr J identified a two-level approach to find economic duress:

1. Did the party asserting the intimidation protest immediately? If yes:
2. Did the party accept the agreement or dispute it openly?

Case:	
***North Ocean Shipping Co. v Hyundai Construction Co. (The Atlantic Baron)* (1979)**	There was a contract for a boat to be built. After building had begun the shipyard increased the price of the boat by 10 per cent, threatening to not finish the boat if the claimants refused to pay. The claimants agreed to pay the increased price because of a charter agreement based on the original completion date. Eight months later the claimants brought an action for the extra money paid. The court accepted that there had been duress of an economic nature but the action failed because of the time it took for the claimants to bring an action.

Case:	
***Pao On v Lau Yiu Long* (1979)**	Unless the defendant agreed to fully subsidise any loss suffered by the claimants in performance of the contract the claimants would not sell their shares. The Privy Council said that the defendants could have used the remedy of specific performance in order to force the claimants to perform their obligations under the contract. Furthermore the evidence suggested nothing more than commercial pressure and thus not economic duress. Lord Scarman, whilst confirming the decision of Kerr J, summarised the conditions for deciding whether economic duress was

	established: *'In determining whether there was a coercion of will such that there was no true consent, it is material to inquire whether the person alleged to have been coerced did or did not protest; whether, at the time he was allegedly coerced into making the contract, he did or did not have an alternative course open to him such as an adequate legal remedy; whether he was independently advised; and whether after entering the contract he took steps to avoid it. All these matters are relevant in determining whether he acted voluntarily or not.'*

The criteria can therefore be summed up as:

1. Did the party claiming to be coerced protest at the time?
2. Was there an alternative option available to the party?
3. Was the party independently advised?
4. After having entered the contract did the party take steps to avoid it?

Workpoint

Considering Lord Scarman's criteria, would you agree that the courts attach more weight to whether there was any realistic alternative for the coerced party than other criteria?

HINT! Consider *Atlas Express Ltd v Kafco (Importers and Distributors) Ltd* (1989).

Research Point

What were the facts of *Universe Tankships Inc. of Monrovia v International Transport Workers' Federation (The Universe Sentinel)* (1983)?

What was the problem with the case and what did it fail to address?

7.2.3.1 Economic duress and lawful/unlawful acts

- Threats of *unlawful* action will, generally speaking, amount to illegitimate pressure.

Case:	
***Atlas Express Ltd v Kafco* (1989)**	Atlas contracted with Kafco to deliver basketwork to Woolworth stores. Because of a miscalculation of the load Atlas increased the cost. Had Kafco not agreed to the increase in price, the contract with Woolworths could have been lost. Kafco accepted the increase but later refused to pay. Atlas brought an action but the court found for Kafco. Tucker J affirmed that Kafco were not bound by the new terms and the new agreement was vitiated. He affirmed that the consent to the agreement was induced by illegitimate pressure. *'Reverting to the case before me, I find that the defendants' apparent consent to the agreement was induced by the pressure which was illegitimate and I find that it was not approbated. In my judgment that pressure can properly be described as economic duress, which is a concept recognised by English law, and which in the circumstances of the present case vitiates the defendants' apparent consent to the agreement.'*

- Threats of *lawful* action may constitute duress if there is no reasonable alternative other than acquiescence for the innocent party.

Case:	
***CTN Cash & Carry v Gallagher* (1994)**	The Court of Appeal held that whilst in certain circumstances a lawful action may constitute duress, on the facts of the case this was not one of them. Gallagher delivered CTN's consignment of cigarettes to the wrong warehouse. Gallagher demanded payment in the honest but mistakenly held belief that CTN's cigarettes were already at CTN's risk under the contract. CTN initially refused to pay up but did so after Gallagher threatened to withdraw CTN's credit facility. CTN then sued claiming the money was only paid under duress. The Court of Appeal held there was no duress where the party issuing the lawful threat (the withdrawal of goods on credit facilities) was a company dealing with another company at arm's length whilst genuinely believing the demand to be valid.

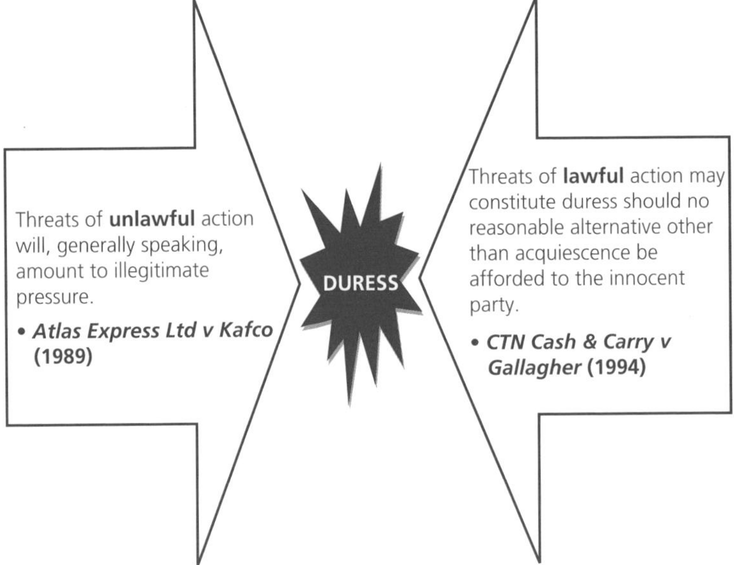

Workpoint

What is the effect of a finding of duress? Use cases to support your answer.

What remedy is available?

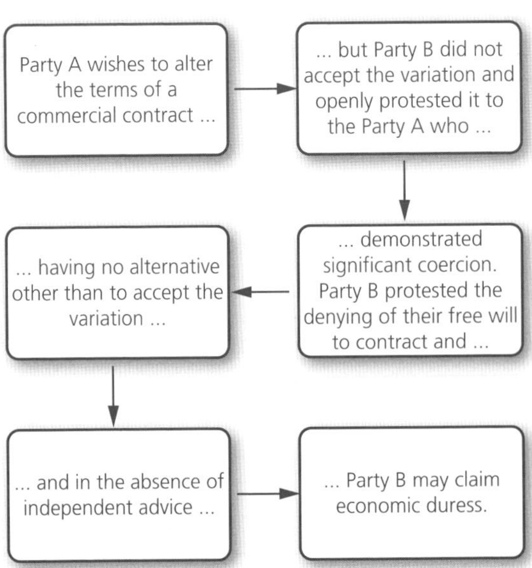

7.3 Undue influence

- Like duress, undue influence will render the contract voidable. The difference being that the doctrine of undue influence concerns itself with **the relationship** between the parties whilst the doctrine of economic duress is concerned with the **threats** made by one party to the other.
- There is no exact definition of undue influence. Lord Scarman in *National Westminster Bank Plc v Morgan* (1985) stated:

'there is no precisely defined law setting limits to the equitable jurisdiction of a court to relieve against undue influence'.

- Lord Clyde, in *Royal Bank of Scotland Plc v Etridge (No. 2)* (2002), said that undue influence:

'... is something which can be more easily recognised when found than when exhaustively examined in the abstract'.

- In *Bank of Credit and Commerce International SA v Abody* (1990) the court defined two classes of undue influence with *Barclays Bank plc v O'Brien* (1993) refining them further.

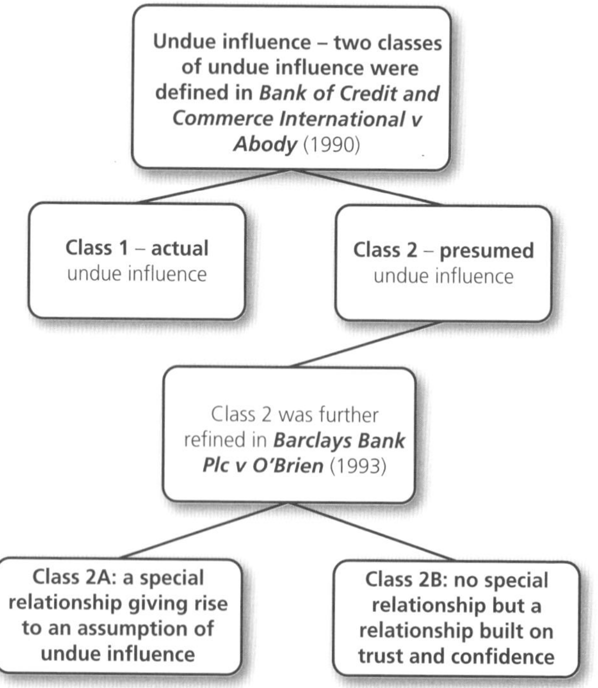

7.3.1 Actual undue influence

- The burden of proof is on the claimant who must prove undue influence was used against them. Where actual undue influence is concerned there is no special relationship and therefore no abuse of confidence.

Case:	
***Williams v Bayley* (1866)**	Facts: A father provided his home as security to prevent his son being prosecuted when a bank discovered that the son had used the father's signature on promissory notes to the bank. Held: The father had not entered the agreement through his own volition. The bank had exerted undue influence.

- In *CIBC Mortgages v Pitt* (1993) the House of Lords rejected the concept that a manifest disadvantage also needed to be proved (*Bank of Credit and Commerce International v Abody* (1990)).

Workpoint

What is the principal difference between the doctrine of economic duress and the doctrine of undue influence?

7.3.2 Presumed undue influence – class 2A – special relationship

- As previously mentioned, *Barclays Bank v O'Brien* refined the criteria for which a presumption of undue influence could be found. A clear explanation of the two classes can be found in *Royal Bank of Scotland plc v Etridge (No. 2)* (2002), class 2A and class 2B.

Class 2A is a presumption based on a special relationship.

- Under the category of class 2A there are two things that need to be proved for presumed undue influence:

1. a special relationship, such as solicitor and client, parent and child; and
2. a transaction that calls for an explanation.

    - Certain special relationships presume influence. *Etridge* affirms that the relationship itself, for example doctor and patient, will prove a non-rebuttable presumption of *influence*. There must be a party exercising influence and a party being influenced.

- If the transaction 'calls for an explanation' or 'is not readily explicable by the relationship of the parties', then there will be a presumption of undue influence.
- The burden of proof shifts to the defendant who must prove that no undue influence was used. Should the defendant be unable to do so, the court will make a finding of undue influence and the contract will be voidable.
- In order to prove there has been no undue influence the defendant must show the following:
  1. the claimant party had independent and impartial advice; and
  2. the claimant knew the full extent and nature of the contract when entering into it.
- It should be noted that any advice must be given with knowledge of all the facts of the case; *Inche Noriah v Shaik Allie Bin Omar* (1929). Furthermore a party may still be acting under undue influence despite knowing the full extent and nature of the transaction at the time of contracting. Lord Nicholls in *Etridge* stated:

'Proof of outside advice does not, of itself, necessarily show that the subsequent completion of the transaction was free from the exercise of undue influence ... so that the transaction was not brought about by the exercise of undue influence, is a question of fact to be decided having regard to all the evidence in the case.'

- Religious leader and disciple:

Case:	
***Allcard v Skinner* (1887)**	Facts: The claimant joined a religious sect. The lady superior was considered the voice of God, all property had to be given to the sect and there was no external advice without the superior's permission. Having left the sect the claimant brought an action for the return of her property. Held: The action was defeated owing to the amount of time (six years) it took for the claimant to bring the action, but nevertheless the Court of Appeal accepted that a presumption of undue influence had arisen.

- Parent and child:

Case:	
***Lancashire Loans Co. v Black* (1933)**	A daughter acted as a guarantor for a loan requested by her mother from a bank. The bank sought to enforce the guarantee given by the daughter when the mother defaulted on payments. The daughter successfully claimed undue influence owing to the fact she did not properly appreciate the nature of what she was signing when entering the agreement, had not received independent advice and was controlled by her mother.

Research Point

A list of some special relationships giving rise to a presumption of undue influence (class 2A) is given below. What are the facts of the cases listed in the table?

Relationship	Case	Facts
Solicitor and client	*Wright v Carter* (1903)	
Doctor and patient	*Dent v Bennett* (1839) 4 My & Cr 269	
Trustee and beneficiary	*Benningfield v Baker* (1886)	

Midland Bank plc v Shephard (1998) specifically excluded husband and wife from the list. There is no automatic presumption of influence between husband and wife.

7.3.3 Presumed undue influence – class 2B – no special relationship

Class 2B covers a relationship from which influence ought to be presumed.

- In the absence of a special relationship between the parties that falls within class 2A and which therefore gives rise to an automatic presumption of undue influence, following *Etridge* where the claimant can show there was a relationship of **trust** and **confidence** and the transaction 'calls for an explanation', a presumption of undue influence arises and the contract may be set aside.

- Like class 2A there must be a party exercising influence and a party being influenced, and the presumption must be rebutted to prevent a finding of undue influence. For class 2B there will be a requirement for a *relationship of trust and confidence* and a transaction which requires an explanation.
- The relationship between husband and wife can fall within this category.

7.4 Undue influence, third parties and the doctrine of notice

- To a large extent cases of undue influence involve coercion by A on B to contract with C for the benefit of A.

- A common scenario might be:

- A delicate balancing act is faced by the courts who often find themselves stuck between trying to protect the spouse from undue influence whilst allowing the bank to be secure in its lending.
- Guidance was found in *Barclays Bank plc v O'Brien* (1994) and through the *doctrine of notice*.

Case:	
***Barclays Bank plc v O'Brien* (1994)**	Facts: Mrs O'Brien was persuaded by Mr O'Brien to sign a guarantee in respect of his overdraft through the granting of a charge as security. Despite the branch manager's request, the bank employee dealing with the matter failed to inform Mrs O'Brien fully about the extent of the agreement, nor did he suggest that it would be sensible for her to obtain independent legal advice. The husband informed his wife that the

	surety was £60,000 when the true amount was £130,000. The bank attempted to enforce the charge when the overdraft was exceeded. Held: The House of Lords allowed Mrs O'Brien to set aside the legal charge on the basis of her being misled by her husband and the bank's failure to fully explain the transaction or recommend taking appropriate independent legal advice. The bank was deemed to have **constructive notice** of the undue influence used by the husband on the wife. The court held that, in certain instances where a person offers security for their spouse's debt, that a creditor should be **put on enquiry** as to undue influence. This will happen where: 1) the transaction is not *prima facie* to the financial advantage of the spouse; and 2) there are substantial risks in transactions of the kind that, in procuring the spouse to act as surety, the individual has committed a legal or equitable wrong that entitles their spouse to set aside the transaction.

- If a creditor is put on enquiry, he or she must ensure that their spouse's agreement to act as surety has been gained appropriately through advice about the agreement's exact nature and the suggestion of seeking independent legal advice. If not, the creditor will be judged to have constructive notice of the spouse's right to have the surety set aside because of undue influence.
- When deciding when the bank is put on enquiry the primary test was formulated by Lord Nicholls in *Royal Bank of Scotland plc v Etridge (No. 2)* (2002):

'… the only practical way forward is to regard banks as "put on enquiry" in every case where the relationship between the surety and the debtor is non-commercial. The creditor must always take reasonable steps to bring home to the individual guarantor the risks he is running by standing as surety.'

- It is clear from this that a bank is 'put on enquiry' when a spouse offers security for an individual's debts. This position is exactly the same for all couples regardless of their sexual orientation. The list was not strictly limited to those of a personal relationship. Lord Nicholls, by using the wider 'non-commercial' principle, left the door open for undue influence to be found in, for example, employment relationships (*Credit Lyonnais Bank Nederland N V v Burch* (1997)).

- When a lender is put on enquiry Lord Nicholls said a bank should take **reasonable steps** in performance of its duty to take reasonable care in protecting the spouse against the risk of undue influence. These reasonable steps include:

  1. Direct communication with the spouse.
  2. The spouse should be informed that the solicitor may also be acting for their husband or wife.
  3. All the necessary financial information needed to best advise the spouse should be provided to the solicitor.
  4. Should the bank suspect undue influence it should inform the solicitor.
  5. The bank should obtain written confirmation that the spouse has received legal advice from the solicitor.

Workpoint

What are the differences between duress and undue influence?

Checkpoint – duress and undue influence

Item on checklist:	**Done!**
I can define duress and the equitable concept of undue influence	
I can explain the different types of undue influence	
I can explain the significance of *Royal Bank of Scotland v Etridge (No. 2)* [2001] HL	
I can differentiate between actual and presumed undue influence	
I can discuss the similarities and differences between duress and undue influence	
I can state how a party may be put on enquiry and how constructive notice may be avoided.	
I can explain the effects of undue influence	

Potential exam questions

1) The courts have fundamentally failed in their attempts to successfully find a happy medium between the requirement to guard those at risk of undue influence and the requirement to

guarantee small businesses the opportunity to borrow from the financial services where the only security is the matrimonial or domestic property.

Discuss.

2) Cheryl is the Member of Parliament for the constituency of Snodgrass. Whilst having an open surgery one Saturday morning Nadine walks in. Nadine is Cheryl's best friend and having been unemployed for six months and facing eviction from her apartment she is now desperate for paid work. Aware that Cheryl is having an affair with Kim, she threatens to tell all to the local newspaper unless Cheryl gives Nadine the cleaning contract for the constituency office.

   There are rumblings amongst the press and halls of Parliament that a general election will be called in the summer. Due to a dip in the polls for Cheryl's party she has not received as much as she had hoped in the way of donations for any re-election campaign. Cheryl persuades her girlfriend Sarah to come with her to the bank and provide her house as security for a loan Cheryl wishes to take out from the White Rose Bank plc. Knowing they have had problems in their relationship and suspecting Cheryl may leave her, Sarah agrees.

   The bank see Cheryl and Sarah that day and in a meeting with the bank Sarah is advised that before pressing ahead she should see a solicitor, who would also see Cheryl, for a 15 minute consultation. During conversation with Sarah the solicitor was distracted by his secretary coming in with messages and emails popping up on his laptop. As a result the solicitor had to leave the office for a meeting before properly explaining the contract and the threat involved with using her house as security.

   Four months after she is re-elected as MP for Snoddygrass Cheryl leaves Sarah for Kim. Extremely bitter, Sarah wishes she had never used her house as security for the loan, especially since Cheryl has said she will not seek re-election at any future general election.

   a) Advise Cheryl as to whether she may have the contract with Nadine set aside.

   b) Advise Sarah as to whether she could avoid the contract with White Rose Bank plc for the use of her house as security.

Chapter 8

Exclusion, exemption and limitation clauses

8.1 Introduction

- Clauses that seek to exclude or limit liability are often found in contracts. Generally speaking they are considered by the courts to be terms of the contract. A common example would be a sign stating 'All items are left at the owner's risk'.
- Ideally there would be equality of bargaining power. This is more common when two businesses of relatively equal standing contract with each other. It is unlikely that the courts will intervene where parties have freely entered into a contract and an exclusion or limitation clause was included as a term.
- Consumers may have little bargaining power when contracting with large organisations. In order to prevent exploitation a mixture of **statutory controls** and **common law rules** have been adopted.

Definition

Limitation clause: The restriction of a party's liability.

Exclusion clause: Where a party is entitled to exclude their liability.

8.2 Exclusion clauses

- It should be noted at this stage that 'exclusion clause' as used in this chapter will cover both exclusion and limitation clauses unless otherwise stated.
- The three stage process which an exclusion clause must pass through in order to be binding:

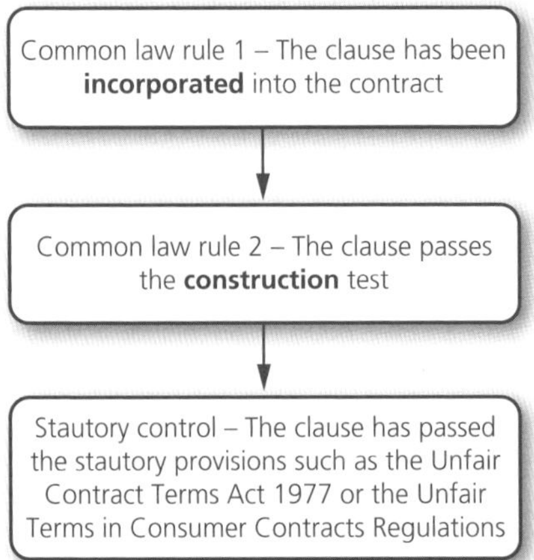

- Where the inclusion of an exclusion clause is in question the common law rules should be applied first and then the statutory controls. Remember that one does not replace the other.

8.3 Stages 1 and 2 – the common law rules

- Two things should be established at common law for an exclusion clause to be valid:

1. The clause must be **incorporated** into the contract (in effect it is a term of the contract); and
2. the clause must pass the **construction** test in that it covers the damage caused and is reasonable.

8.3.1 The clause must be incorporated into the contract

- Generally, as with the inclusion of terms, a party will be bound by the terms if they have been incorporated into the contract. An exclusion clause may be incorporated in one of three ways:

1. signature
2. notice
3. course of dealings.

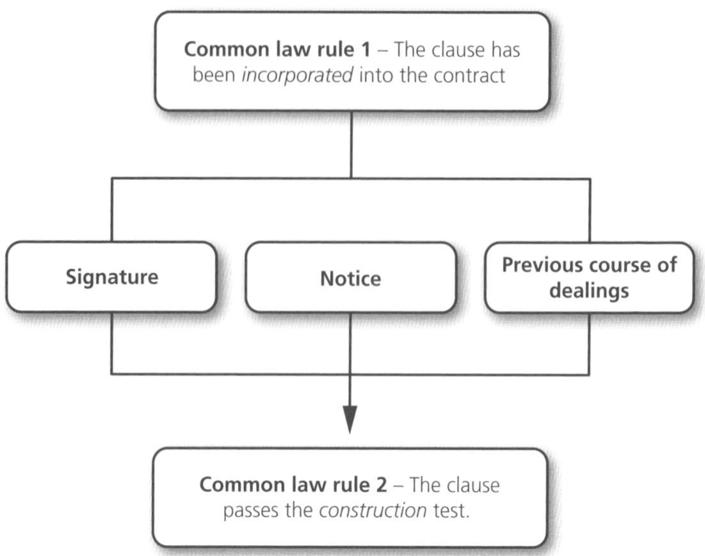

8.3.1.1 Signature

- If a party signs a contract they will normally be bound by its terms and exclusion clauses whether or not the contract has been read.

Case:	
***L'Estrange v Graucob* (1934)**	Facts: The claimant bought a vending machine from the defendant and signed a sales agreement containing an exclusion clause freeing the defendant from liability should the vending machine be faulty. Held: the defendant was able to rely on the exclusion clause when the machine proved to be faulty even though the claimant did not read the contract before signing.

- If there is a misrepresentation then the defendant cannot always rely on an exclusion clause.

Case:	
***Curtis v Chemical Cleaning and Dyeing Co. Ltd* (1951)**	Facts: The claimant took a wedding dress to a dry cleaner. The claimant having signed a receipt asked about its contents. The sales assistant informed the claimant that there was an exclusion clause excluding the defendant from liability should any damage 'howsoever caused' occur, but that the clause **only** referred to damage caused to sequins or beads. The dress was stained during the cleaning process.

	Held: The claimant could claim damages. The sales assistant's statement meant that the defendant could not rely on the exclusion clause.

Workpoint

What is the difference between an exclusion clause and a limitation clause?

8.3.1.2 Notice

- A clause may be incorporated into a contract through notice where the document has not been signed. A party who is subject to an exclusion clause must have knowledge of its existence, though not necessarily its contents.
- An exclusion clause may not be relied on by a party if the other party is not aware of the clause.

8.3.1.2.1 Timing of the notice

- The exclusion clause must be brought to the attention of the party that will be subject to it at the time or before the contract is made.

Case:	
***Olley v Marlborough Court Hotel* (1949)**	Facts: A contract for a stay at a hotel was formed at the point of check-in. The claimants went out for the evening and left their room key with reception. Whilst the claimants were out the key was taken by a third party who used it to gain access to the claimants' room where a fur coat was stolen. The claimant sued the hotel. The defendant sought to rely on the following exclusion clause: 'The proprietors will not hold themselves liable for articles lost or stolen unless handed to the manager for safe custody.' Held: The defendant could not rely on the exclusion clause as it could not have been incorporated into the contract. At the time of the contract's formation the claimants were unaware of the exclusion clause (notice).

- The notice must be adequate and the party incorporating the exclusion clause has responsibility for bringing it to the attention of the other party. Should they fail to do so, before or at the time of the contract formation, they will not be free of liability for any breach of contract.
- The more unusual or difficult the clause, the greater the degree of notice that will be required (*Spurling v Bradshaw* (1956)). This is referred to as the **'red hand rule'**. In *Spurling* Denning LJ stated:

'The more unreasonable a clause is, the greater the degree of notice which must be given of it. Some clauses I have seen would need to be printed in red ink on the face of the document with a red hand pointing to it before the notice could be held to be sufficient.'

Case:	
***Thornton v Shoe Lane Parking* (1971)**	Facts: The claimant took a ticket from a machine upon arrival at a car park. On the ticket was a clause stating that the ticket was issued subject to conditions. When the claimant drove into the car park he then noticed signs stating that the owners of the car park were not liable for any personal injury sustained whilst in the car park. The claimant, owing to the negligence of the defendants, suffered personal injury. Held: The defendants could not rely on the exclusion clause. The existence of the clause was not brought sufficiently to the attention of the claimant before the contract was made.

8.3.1.2.2 What contains the clause must be contractual in nature

Case:	
***Parker v South Eastern Railway Co.* (1877)**	Facts: The defendant gave the claimant a ticket after taking his luggage at a cloakroom. On the ticket was the word, 'back'. On the back of the ticket the company had written that they would not be liable should an item exceed £10 in value. Held: The claimant's luggage was worth more than this amount but he was still able to bring an action

	for compensation when his luggage was stolen. The defendants unsuccessfully sought to rely on the exclusion clause. The Court of Appeal asserted that only 'reasonably sufficient steps' should be taken to bring the exclusion clause to the claimant's attention.

Research Point

What were the questions put to the jury by Mellish LJ in the Court of Appeal during *Parker v South Eastern Railway*?

- Following *Parker* an exclusion clause will only have been incorporated if it is within a document that can be considered to contain contractual terms or be legally binding.

Research Point

Considering incorporation by notice, why did the claimant's action fail in *Thompson v London Midland and Scottish Railway Co.* (1930)?

Why was the case decided differently to that of *Thornton v Shoe Lane Parking* (1971) considering both cases are factually similar?

Case:	
Chapelton v Barry Urban District Council **(1940)**	Facts: The claimant received a ticket having paid for the rental of two deck chairs. The claimant did not read the ticket. On the reverse of the ticket was an exclusion clause absolving the council of liability for any injury caused as a result of hiring the chairs. When the claimant was injured using the chairs he sued the council for damages. Held: The claim was successful. The clause was not successfully brought to the attention of the claimant. The ticket was not a contractual document and it would be wrong to assume a reasonable person would think it was.

8.3.1.2.3 Incorporation owing to a previous course of dealings

An exception to the rules on sufficient notice on the inclusion of clauses is where the parties have engaged previously. Despite not knowing of an exclusion clause in a current business deal, a party will be deemed to have had notice of an exclusion clause if it has been sufficiently brought to their attention in previous dealings.

- There are two requirements for a court to assume incorporation as a result of previous dealings, namely:
  1. consistency during the course of previous dealings
  2. regularity of previous dealings.

Case:	
***J Spurling Ltd v Bradshaw* (1956)**	Facts: There had been dealings for many years over the storage of goods at a warehouse. On a particular occasion the claimant took receipt of eight barrels of orange juice and the next day sent a letter to the defendant confirming this. The letter also contained a clause denying liability should the goods be lost or damaged. The defendant refused to pay the storage charges when he went to collect the barrels and found them empty and damaged. The claimant brought an action for breach of contract. Held: Despite the fact that the document containing the exclusion clause was not received until after the contract was formed, the court allowed its incorporation. As part of previous dealings the defendant had been in receipt of the exclusion clause and never read it, nor sought to have it altered or amended.

- The previous course of dealings must have been consistent.

Case:	
***McCutcheon v David MacBrayne* (1964)**	Facts: a claimant had sometimes been asked to sign a 'risk note', which referred to an exclusion clause for the transportation of a car by ferry, and sometimes not. Due to the negligence of the defendant the claimant's car was written off when the ship sank. On this occasion he had not been asked to sign a 'risk note'.

	Held: There had not been a consistent approach during the course of dealings and they were not prepared to infer the clause.

Workpoint

Are 'three or four occasions over the past five years' enough for the incorporation of a term due to previous dealings? (Consider *Hollier v Rambler Motors (AMC) Ltd* (1972).)

8.3.2 The clause must pass the test of construction

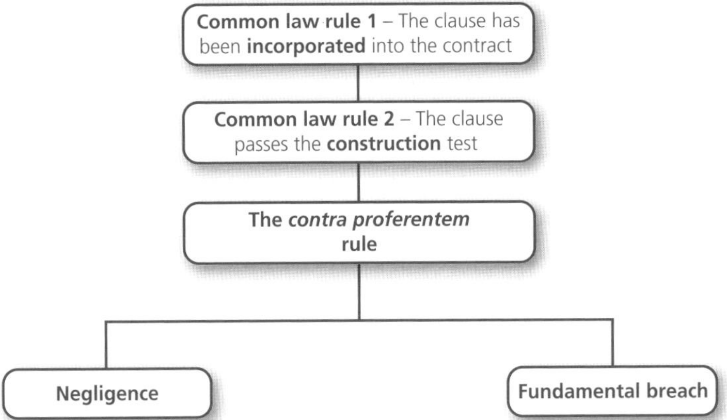

Definition

Contra preferentem: An exemption clause is interpreted against the party that inserted it into the contract and seeks to rely upon it.

- Despite the fact that an exclusion clause has been successfully incorporated, it is still possible that the party that inserted the clause may not use it to avoid liability. The clause must still pass the test of construction.

Case:	
***Andrews Bros (Bournemouth) Ltd v Singer and Co.* (1934)**	Facts: A contract was agreed to purchase 'new Singer cars'. Under the terms of the agreement an exclusion clause provided that 'all conditions, warranties and liabilities implied by statute, common law or otherwise'. One of the cars delivered by the defendant was second hand. Held: The car dealer could not rely on the exclusion clause since it only excluded liability for implied terms. The term 'new' was an express term.

- *A fundamental breach* – an exclusion clause will be ineffective where it seeks to exclude liability for a fundamental breach of contract no matter how clearly worded the clause was. However the House of Lords rejected the 'fundamental breach' doctrine in *Photo Productions Ltd v Securicor Transport Ltd* (1980). *Internet Broadcasting Corporation Ltd v Mar LLC* (2010) confirmed that an exclusion clause will not protect a party from loss of profit as a result of a deliberate denial of contractual responsibility.
- *Exempting liability in negligence* – an exclusion clause may attempt to exclude liability for negligence. Should it do so there must be no ambiguity and specific language must be used. A specific reference to 'negligence' is usually required in the exclusion clause.

Case:	
***Hollier v Rambler Motors (AMC) Ltd* (1972)**	Facts: The claimant left his car at the defendant's garage. As a result of the defendant's negligence, a fire broke out at the garage and destroyed the claimant's car. The contract between the two parties contained a term that stated 'the company is not responsible for damage caused by fire to customers' cars on the premises'. Held: The garage could not rely on the exclusion clause as it ought to have cleared up any ambiguity by stating that it would not be liable for its own negligence.

Research Point

What other factors limit the effectiveness of exemption clauses?

What is the effect of exemption clauses on third parties to the contract?

Research Point

What are the legal principles derived from the following cases?

1) *L'Estrange v Graucob* (1934)
2) *Olley v Marlborough Court Hotel* (1949)
3) *J Spurling v Bradshaw* (1956)
4) *Dillon v Baltic Shipping Co. Ltd (The Mikhail Lermontov)* (1991)
5) *Karsales (Harrow) Ltd v Wallis* (1956)

8.4 Stage 3 – statutory control of exemption clauses

- The final hurdle that an exclusion clause must overcome in order to become binding is that of statutory provisions. The statutory limitation and control of exemption clauses is nothing new as the following table shows:

Statute	Limitation of exemption clause
• s 151 Road Traffic Act 1960 (now contained in s 29 of the Public Passenger Vehicles Act 1981)	It is not permitted for a person to limit or negate liability for the death or injury of a passenger getting out of or being carried in a public vehicle.
• s 149 Road Traffic Act 1988	A user of a motor vehicle is not permitted to restrict, negate or impose conditions on liability in respect of a passenger.
• s 3 Misrepresentation Act 1967	The limitation or exclusion of liability owing to misrepresentation will only be accepted by a court if it is fair and reasonable.

For the purpose of exclusion clauses the most commonly used legislation is:

- the Unfair Contract Terms Act 1977 (commonly referred to as 'UCTA')
- the Unfair Terms in Consumer Contracts Regulations 1999.

8.4.1 The Unfair Contract Terms Act 1977 – 'UCTA'

- Legislation has now overtaken the common law as the most efficient way of managing exclusion clauses.
- UCTA limits the extent to which liability may be excluded or restricted for negligence or breach of contract. It seeks to protect the consumer through equalling the bargaining strength. The title of the Act is somewhat misleading since it is not concerned with whether the terms of a contract are 'fair'. It relatess to terms that seek to exclude or limit liability.
- As a result of UCTA an exclusion clause may:
  1. be declared **void**
  2. be subject to a test of **reasonableness**.
- Ss 2–7 of the Act only applies to '**business liability**'.
- s1 (3) states:

> *'In the case of both contract and tort, sections 2 to 7 apply (except where the contrary is stated in section 6(4)) only to business liability, that is liability for breach of obligations or duties arising —*
>
> *(a) from things done or to be done by a person in the course of a business (whether his own business or another's); or*
>
> *(b) from the occupation of premises used for business purposes of the occupier;'*

- '**Business**' includes professions, government departments and local authorities because of the wide definition given at s 14 of 'business' as:

> *'including a profession and the activities of any government department or public authority'.*
>
> *Therefore the contract negotiated between two individuals would not be covered by UCTA except for:*
>
> *(1) UCTA s 6 – implied terms in sale of goods and hire-purchase contracts;*
>
> *(2) UCTA s 7 – implied terms in the supply of goods and services contracts;*
>
> *(3) UCTA s 8 – misrepresentation.*

- As mentioned above, one of the main aims of the Act is the protection of any person who 'deals as a consumer', s 12 provides:

> *'(1) A party to a contract "deals as consumer" in relation to another party if —*
>
> *(a) he neither makes the contract in the course of a business nor holds himself out as doing so; and*
>
> *(b) the other party does make the contract in the course of a business; and*
>
> *(c) in the case of a contract governed by the law of sale of goods or hire-purchase, or by section 7 of this Act, the goods passing under or in pursuance of the contract are of a type ordinarily supplied for private use or consumption.*

> *(1A) But if the first party mentioned in subsection (1) is an individual paragraph (c) of that subsection must be ignored.*
>
> *(2) But the buyer is not in any circumstances to be regarded as dealing as consumer —*
>
> *(a) if he is an individual and the goods are second hand goods sold at public auction at which individuals have the opportunity of attending the sale in person;*

> *(b) if he is not an individual and the goods are sold by auction or by competitive tender.*
>
> *(3) Subject to this, it is for those claiming that a party does not deal as consumer to show that he does not.'*

- The act does not extend to all kinds of contracts. Schedule 1 of the act lists these as:

  '(a) any contract of insurance (including a contract to pay an annuity on human life);

  (b) any contract so far as it relates to the creation or transfer of an interest in land;

  (c) any contract so far as it relates to the creation or transfer of a right or interest in any patent, trade mark, copyright registered design, technical or commercial information or other intellectual property, or relates to the termination of any such right or interest;

  (d) the formation or dissolution of a company (which means any body corporate or unincorporated association and includes a partnership), or

  (e) any contract so far as it relates to the creation or transfer of securities or of any right or interest in securities;

  (f) any contract of marine salvage or towage;

  (g) any charter party of a ship or hovercraft; and

  (h) any contract for the carriage of goods by ship or hovercraft; but subject to this sections 2 to 4 and 7 do not extend to any such contract except in favour of a person dealing as consumer.'

Workpoint

List five examples of a party 'dealing as a consumer'.

8.4.1.1 Exclusion and limitation clauses rendered void by the Unfair Contract Terms Act 1977

Certain exclusion and limitation clauses are rendered void by the Act regardless of whether they have been successfully incorporated into the contract or not. Invalid exclusions include those relating to:

1. *Negligence – s 2(1)*. A party may not exclude or limit liability for injury or death caused by negligence.

2. *Guarantee of consumer goods – s 5(1)*. Manufacturers will not be permitted to limit or exclude liability as a result of product guarantees.

3. *Sale and hire-purchase*

   - *s 6(1)*. The implied promise regarding title that is contained in s 12 of the Sale of Goods Act 1979 may not be subject to exclusion or restriction.
   - *s 6(2)*. In any consumer contract it is not permitted to have exclusion clauses avoiding liability for breaches of implied conditions relating to quality, description, fitness for purpose (ss 13–15 Sale of Goods Act 1979).

4. *Contracts under which goods pass – s 7(1)*. Goods that are transferred under the Supply of Goods and Services Act 1982 mirror the principles which apply in s 6.

5. *Consumer Protection Act 1987 – s 7*. Product liability may not be excluded or limited by any contractual notice, term or other provision. It states:

> *'The liability of a person by virtue of this Part to a person who has suffered damage caused wholly or partly by a defect in a product, or to a dependant or relative of such a person, shall not be limited or excluded by any contract term, by any notice or by any other provision.'*

Case:	
***R and B Customs Brokers Co. Ltd v United Dominions Trust Ltd* (1988)**	Facts: Mr and Mrs Bell were the owners of a private shipping brokers' firm. They purchased a car for one of the company directors with the car to be used partly for business and partly for private use. Held: The Court of Appeal held that since the normal activities of the business were nothing to do with the buying and selling of cars, the company was acting as a consumer and therefore they had a consumer contract.

Workpoint

Why has the decision of the Court of Appeal in *R and B Customs Brokers Co. Ltd v United Dominions Trust Ltd* (1988) been so heavily criticised?

HINT! *Davies v Sumner* (1984)/Trade Descriptions Act 1968.

Research Point

What was the effect of *Stevenson v Rogers* (1999) on the definition of 'in the course of business'?

What point did Potter LJ make in respect of *R and B Custom Brokers*?

8.4.1.2 Exclusion clauses subject to the test of reasonableness (Unfair Contract Terms Act 1977)

- As a result of s 11(1) Unfair Contract Terms Act 1977 a test of reasonableness will be applied to certain exclusion clauses. What is deemed reasonable is defined by s 11(1) as:

> *'In relation to a contract term, the requirement of reasonableness for the purposes of this Part of this Act, section 3 of the Misrepresentation Act 1967 and section 3 of the Misrepresentation Act (Northern Ireland) 1967 is that the term shall have been a fair and reasonable one to be included having regard to the circumstances which were, or ought reasonably to have been, known to or in the contemplation of the parties when the contract was made.'*

- The party that wants to rely on the clause has the burden of proving its reasonableness, *Warren v Truprint Ltd* (1986).
- If the clause does not satisfy the test of reasonableness then the entire clause fails.
- The court will look at the guidance given in Schedule 2 of the Act for the application of the reasonableness test.
- The guidelines for the test of reasonableness in Schedule 2 of the Act state:

> *'The matters to which regard is to be had in particular for the purposes of sections 6(3), 7(3) and (4), 20 and 21 are any of the following which appear to be relevant —*

> *(a) the strength of the bargaining positions of the parties relative to each other, taking into account (among other things) alternative means by which the customer's requirements could have been met;*
>
> *(b) whether the customer received an inducement to agree to the term, or in accepting it had an opportunity of entering into a similar contract with other persons, but without having a similar term;*
>
> *(c) whether the customer knew or ought reasonably to have known of the existence and the extent of the term (having regard, among other things, to any custom of the trade and any previous course of dealing between the parties);*
>
> *(d) where the term excludes or restricts any relevant liability if some condition was not complied with, whether it was reasonable at the time of the contract to expect that compliance with that condition would be practicable;*
>
> *(e) whether the goods were manufactured, processed or adapted to the special order of the customer.'*

Definition

Dealing as a consumer: S 12 says that a party will be dealing as a consumer if they do not make the contract in the course of business nor pretend to do so.

'In the course of business': The decision in *R and B Customs Brokers Co. Ltd v United Dominions Trust Ltd* means the transaction must be an essential part of the business.

- The test in s 11 for reasonableness applies to the following sections:

1. *Negligence – s 2(2)*. Liability cannot be excluded for loss or damage that is not related to personal injury or death.
2. *Liability for breach of contract – s 3*. Unless it is reasonable, a party cannot rely on its own inclusion of an exclusion clause for breach of contract: where there was no performance or a substantially different performance, where one party dealt as a consumer, or on standard forms.

3. *Indemnity* – s 4. A person dealing as a consumer will be subject to the test of reasonableness if they wish to indemnify another person for breach of contract or negligence.
4. *Sale of goods and hire purchases* – s 6(3). An attempt to limit or exclude liability of implied terms contained in sections 13, 14(2) and (3) and 15 of the Sale of Goods Act 1979 (for those not acting as a consumer) and sch 4 para 5 of the Consumer Credit Act 1974, will be subject to the concept of reasonableness.
5. *Transfer of goods and hire contract* – s 7(3) sets out where in the course of business there is a breach of implied conditions in the Supply of Goods and Services Act 1982 ss 3–5.
6. *Misrepresentation* – s 8. The test of reasonableness will apply to any contractual term that seeks to limit or exclude liability for misrepresentation.

- A more lenient approach is applied to reasonableness for limitation clauses. S 11(4) requires the court to look at the following:

> *'Where by reference to a contract term or notice a person seeks to restrict liability to a specified sum of money, and the question arises (under this or any other Act) whether the term or notice satisfies the requirement of reasonableness, regard shall be had in particular (but without prejudice to subsection (2) above in the case of contract terms) to —*
>
> *(a) the resources which he could expect to be available to him for the purpose of meeting the liability should it arise; and*
>
> *(b) how far it was open to him to cover himself by insurance.'*

Workpoint

Which sections of the Unfair Contracts Terms Act 1977 make clauses void for mistake?

Workpoint

Who is affected by the Unfair Contract Terms Act 1977?

Workpoint

What factors should the court consider when considering the test of reasonableness?

- The Unfair Contract Terms Act 1997 does **not** apply to all contracts. It includes, but is not limited to, contracts concerning:
  - insurance contracts
  - land interests
  - the creation or transfer of intellectual property rights
  - formation or dissolution of companies
  - transfer of securities.

8.4.2 The Unfair Terms in Consumer Contracts Regulations 1999

- The Unfair Terms in Consumer Contracts Regulations 1999 brought the Unfair Terms in Consumer Contracts EC Directive (93/13) into domestic law on 1st October 1999.
- The Regulations are both broader and narrower than UCTA. On the one hand they only apply to consumer contracts with a consumer being defined as a 'natural person'. On the other hand the Regulations are broader in the sense that they don't just aim to control exclusion or limitation clauses but unfair terms generally.

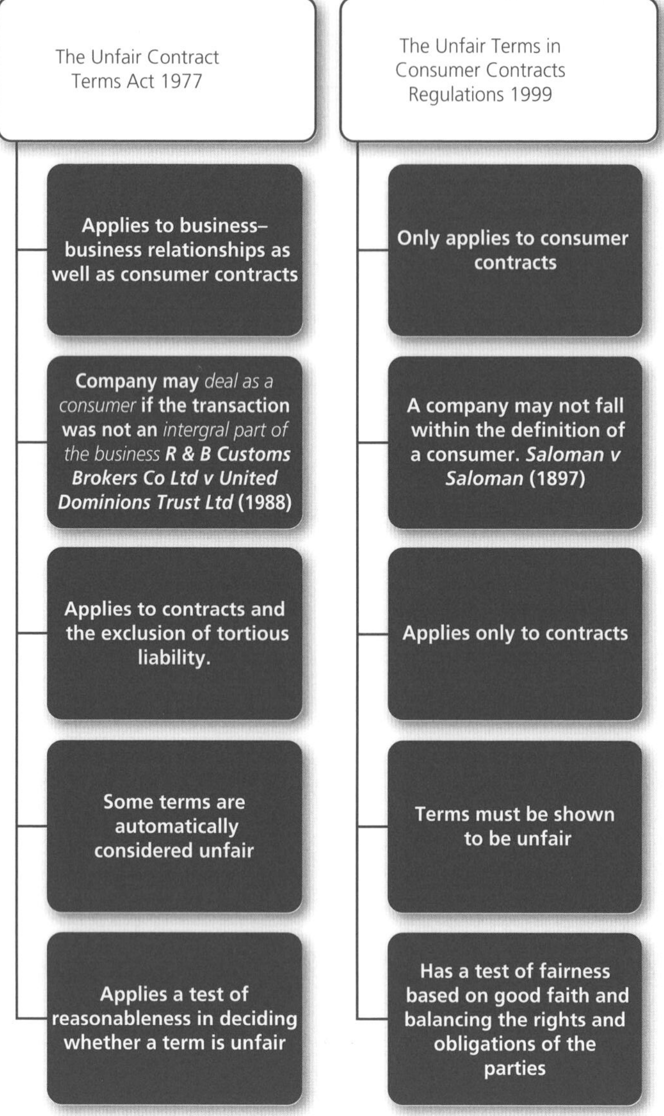

8.4.2.1 The requirement of 'good faith'

- The Regulations state that an unfair term is:

> *'contrary to the requirement of good faith and causes a significant imbalance in the parties' rights and obligations under the contract to the detriment of the consumer'.*

- Sch 2 of the Regulations (1994) sets out that in order for good faith to be established, the following factors would be considered:

> *'Schedule 2 to the regulations provides:*
>
> - *In making an assessment of good faith, regard shall be had in particular to:*
>
>   *(a) the strength of the bargaining positions of the parties;*
>
>   *(b) whether the consumer had an inducement to agree to the term;*
>
>   *(c) whether the goods or services were sold or supplied to the special order of the consumer; and*
>
>   *(d) the extent to which the seller or supplier has dealt fairly and equitably with the consumer.'*

Research Point

In Schedule 2 of the Unfair Terms in Consumer Contracts Regulations 1999 what examples of unfair terms are given?

- Lord Bingham in *Director General of Fair Trading v First National Bank plc* (2002) considered the list of unfair terms in Schedule 2 of the Regulations to be a very good list. He commented on good faith:

'The requirement of good faith in this context is one of fair and open dealing. Openness requires that terms should be expressed fully, clearly and legibly, containing no pitfalls or traps. Appropriate prominence should be given to terms which might operate disadvantageously to the customer. Fair dealing requires that a supplier should not, whether deliberately or unconsciously, take advantage of the consumer's necessity, indigence, lack of experience, unfamiliarity with the subject matter of the contract, weak bargaining position or any other factor listed in or analogous to those listed in Schedule 2 of the Regulations.'

Research Point

What has the Law Commission recently proposed in this area of law?

HINT! Law Com No. 292, Unfair Terms in Contracts, CM 6464

Checkpoint – exclusion and limitation clauses

Item on checklist:	Done!
I can state the three-stage process which an exclusion clause must pass in order to be binding	
I can define exclusion and limitation clauses giving clear examples	
I can state how an exclusion clause may be incorporated into a contract	
I can state the difference between an exclusion and limitation clause	
I can explain the significance of *Parker v South Eastern Railway Co.* (1877) 2 CPD 416	
I can explain the significance of *Shogun Finance Ltd v Hudson* [2004] 1 All ER 215	
I can draw a diagram illustrating the stage of 'construction'	
I can explain the impact of UCTA 1977 on exclusion clauses	

Potential exam questions

The Unfair Contract Terms Act 1977 and Unfair Terms in Consumer Contracts Regulations 1999 both, to an extent, govern contracts. What problems may this cause? Assess whether the Law Commission's proposals solve these.

Chapter 9
Discharge of contracts

9.1 Introduction

- A party is bound by obligations under a contract. Obligations end when a contract is discharged. If a contract is discharged it therefore means the contract has ended. A contract may be discharged in four ways.

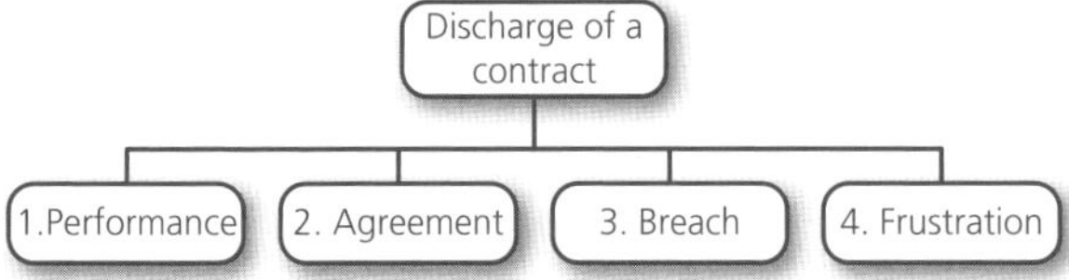

9.2 Performance

- If the parties perform their obligations under the contract then the contract shall be completed and therefore discharged.
- If a party fails to perform their obligations under the 'entire' contract then they may be liable for breach of contract and the innocent party may be entitled to remedies. The contract would not be 'discharged' because a party has not met its obligations and there has not been a full performance of their obligations.

Definition

De minimis non curat lex: The law does not concern itself with trifles or microscopic deviations.

Research Point

Had the contract been 'performed' in *Re Moore & Co. v Landauer & Co.* [1921] 2 KB 519?

Case:	
***Cutter v Powell* (1756)**	Facts: A widow sued for her late husband's wages. He was a seaman who died en route and technically failed to keep his side of the bargain (completing the voyage). Held: The court refused the wife's claim on the basis the performance by her husband had not been completed.

Case:	
***Arcos Ltd v E A Ronaasen & Son* (1933)**	A contract was made for a consignment of wooden staves half an inch thick. The staves delivered were nine-sixteenths thick. The House of Lords held that despite the extra sixteenth making no difference to how useful the staves would have been, the purchaser was permitted to reject the shipment. Lord Atkin suggested that the law does not concern itself with minor or minimal deviations (*de minimis non curat lex*) **unless** precise performance is specifically required.

- The harshness of the strict performance rule has encouraged criticism. Lord Wilberforce in *Reardon Smith Line Ltd v Yngvar Hansen-Tangen* (1976) called the decisions in *Landauer* and *Ronaasen* and many decisions on Sale of Goods contracts 'excessively technical'.
- There are statutory implications in this area as the list below shows:
  - Sale of Goods Act 1979 s 30(1–2) supports the strict approach:

> *(1) 'Where the seller delivers to the buyer a quantity of goods less than he contracted to sell, the buyer may reject them, but if the buyer accepts the goods so delivered he must pay for them at the contract rate.'*
>
> *and*
>
> *(2) 'Where the seller delivers to the buyer a quantity of goods larger than he contracted to sell, the buyer may accept the goods included in the contract and reject the rest, or he may reject the whole.'*

- Sale of Goods Act 1979 s 30(2A) (as inserted by s 4(2) Sale and Supply of Goods Act 1994) provides a statutory basis for the *de minimis rule* in non-consumer contracts.

> (2A) *'A buyer who does not deal as consumer may not —*
>
> *(a) where the seller delivers a quantity of goods less than he contracted to sell, reject the goods under subsection (1) above, or*
>
> *(b) where the seller delivers a quantity of goods larger than he contracted to sell, reject the whole under subsection (2) above,*
>
> *if the shortfall or, as the case may be, excess is so slight that it would be unreasonable for him to do so.*
>
> *(2B) It is for the seller to show that a shortfall or excess fell within subsection (2A) above.'*

- Sale of Goods Act 1979 s 15A (as inserted by s 4(1) Sale and Supply of Goods Act 1994) stops a buyer from rejecting a consignment of goods that only differ slightly from the description given in the contract.

Workpoint

Do you agree with Lord Wilbeforce's comments that the decisions in *Landauer* and *Ronaasen* and the many decisions on Sale of Goods contracts are 'excessively technical'?

- Given the persistent criticism of the strict performance rule and the seemingly unfair decisions, the courts have now developed exceptions to the rule.

9.2.1 Exceptions to the strict performance rule

There are considered to be six exceptions to the strict performance rule:

- *Divisible contracts* – If a contract consists of the performance of several obligations which can be divided up into various stages, a party can insist on payment for obligations that have been completed even if there are outstanding obligations that are still to be performed. This is not unusual in the building industry where staggered payments are common.
- *Partial performance* – A party can accept partial performance by another (*Christy v Row* (1808)) instead of substantial performance. Payment can be made on a *quantum meruit* basis for the work completed. There must be a genuine choice to accept partial performance. Partial performance is supported by the Sale of Goods Act 1979 s 30(1).

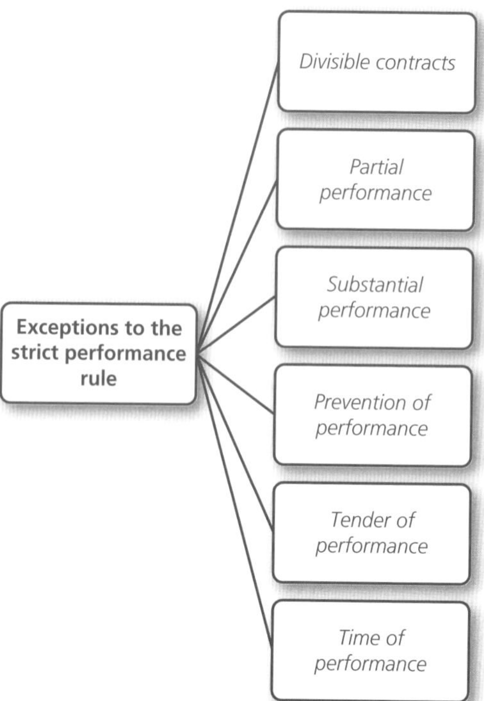

Case:	
***Sumpter v Hedges* (1898)**	The claimant completed about two thirds of the work on land belonging to the defendant before disappearing. As a result the defendant completed the building work himself. The claimant's action for *quantum meruit* failed because the defendant had no choice but to accept partial performance.

Definition

Quantum meruit: Payment for the work done. Latin: 'as much as is deserved'.

- *Substantial performance* – A party that has performed most of what the contract required may get a payment that is representative of the work completed, usually the contract price minus the cost of completing the contract).

Case:	
***Hoenig v Isaacs* (1952)**	The claimant agreed to decorate the defendant's flat for £750. The claimant sued for the balance after the defendant only paid £400 because they claimed the workmanship was poor. The court agreed the workmanship was poor but said it could be resolved for £55. The claimant was awarded £295: the cost of the contract (£750) less money already paid (£400) and the cost of correcting the defects (£55).

Research Point

Which exceptions to the strict performance rule do the following cases relate to?

1) *Taylor v Webb* (1937)
2) *Sumpter v Hedges* (1898)
3) *Startup v Macdonald* (1843)
4) *Bolton v Mahadeva* (1972)
5) *Hoenig v Isaacs* (1952)
6) *Planche v Colburn* (1831)

- *Prevention of performance* – The strict rule will not apply where one party prevents another party from carrying out its obligations. The innocent party can recover damages on a *quantum meruit* basis, *Planche v Colbourn* (1831).
- *Tender of performance* – A party will make an offer to tender where it was unable to complete performance due to the other party unjustly refusing to accept performance. If a party refuses the offer of tender the other party will be released from its responsibilities under the contract. The tender of performance is as good as performance.

Case:	
***Startup v Macdonald* (1843)**	Facts: The claimant delivered 10 tons of linseed oil on 31st March at 8.30 pm which the defendant refused to accept or pay for. It had been agreed that the oil would be delivered by the end of March. Held: The claim was successful and the claimant could claim damages for the non-acceptance. The tender of performance was equivalent to performance.

Research Point

Why might *Startup v Macdonald* (1843) be decided differently today?

- *Time of performance* – Where 'time is of the essence' (vital to the contract) rejection of the contract will be possible in three circumstances:

  1. The contract specifically states time is of the essence.
  2. The circumstances and characteristics of the contract, for example perishable foods, suggest time is of the essence.
  3. Where one party fails to perform and the other party states the performance needs to take place within a certain time.

9.3 Discharge by agreement

- A contract is formed through agreement and a new agreement supported by a consideration will also end an agreement. A contract may be discharged **bilaterally** or **unilaterally**.

Definition

Bilateral discharge: Both parties gain from the new agreement to discharge.

Unilateral discharge: One party releases the other from their obligations and therefore one party benefits from the discharge.

- An agreement by both parties to end the contract will be sufficient consideration. Where an agreement is unilaterally discharged a fresh consideration or a deed will be needed to release a party from their obligations under the contract.

9.4 Discharge by breach

- Where a party fails to perform its responsibilities under a contract they are said to be in breach of contract. A breach may also occur where a party states they no longer wish or intend to fulfil their responsibilities under the contract.

Definition

Fundamental breach: This is also known as a *repudiatory* breach of contract. It is so serious that it allows the innocent party to terminate performance of the contract and pursue a claim for damages.

Anticipatory breach: This is a statement by one of the parties to the contract that they do not intend to complete some or all of their obligations or responsibilities under the contract. This may be implied by conduct.

9.4.1 Termination

- An innocent party may be able to terminate the contract and pursue a claim for damages if the other party has failed to perform their obligations under the contract.
- If a contract is terminated future obligations need not be performed, but this is not the case for obligations already carried out.
- *Fundamental breach* – refers to a breach of a non-conditional term that has the effect of being so serious that the innocent party has the right of repudiation. Lord Reid in *Suisse Atlantique Societe d'Armement Maritime SA v NV Rotterdamsche Kolen Centrale* (1966) defined fundamental breach as a:

  '*well-known type* of breach which entitles the innocent party to treat it as repudiatory and to rescind the contract'.

Lord Greene MR in *Alderslade v Hendon Laundry Ltd* (1945) called the fundamental term 'the hard core of the contract'.

- *Anticipatory breach* – refers to when a party puts the other party on notice before the date of performance of the contract (*Hochster v De La Tour* (1853)). It can also be inferred from their conduct (*Frost v Knight* (1872)) that they are unwilling or unable to complete their responsibilities under the contract. In these circumstances the innocent party may:

  1. accept the repudiation of the other party, thus releasing both parties from future obligations under the contract, and then pursue a claim for damages; or
  2. affirm (continue) the contract until the other party breaches the contract and then claim for damages. If a party affirms they will not then be permitted to terminate the contract at a later date. A delay in accepting the breach by the innocent party may result in a loss of the right to sue for breach of contract (*Avery v Bowden* (1855)).

Research Point

What are the facts of:

1) *Hochster v De La Tour* (1853);
2) *Frost v Knight* (1872) ?

Workpoint

What is the difference between the remedies available for a breach of condition and a breach of warranty?

9.4.2 The effect of a breach

- Termination of the contract is a right given only where there is a breach of essential terms that lie at the heart of the contract (**conditions**) or breaches of innominate terms (terms which are **fundamental**). Breaches of minor terms (**warranties**) will allow a party to claim for damages but not repudiation.
- So the innocent party may be entitled to claim the following remedies:

  1. damages;
  2. specific performance;
  3. termination of the contract and

  which remedy will depend on whether there was

  a) a breach of **condition**; or
  b) a breach of **warranty**; or
  c) a fundamental breach of an **innominate** term.

Breach	Explanation	Remedy
A breach of *condition*	The breach of an **important** term that goes to the heart of the contract. The innocent party must accept the breach.	The innocent party may choose to: • Repudiate (cancel) the contract effective from the date of the breach. • Claim damages for the non-performance of obligations after the date of repudiation. • Affirm (continue) the contract and perhaps later claim for damages.

Breach	Explanation	Remedy
A breach of *warranty*	The breach of a **minor** term or where the breach is not serious and repudiation is unjustifiable.	Caution should be exercised here. An attempt to repudiate may in itself be a breach of contract. Nevertheless an innocent party may pursue a claim for damages where there has been a breach of warranty.
A breach on an *innominate* term	A term that may be considered either a condition or warranty.	The innocent party may: • Repudiate the contract and claim for damages. • Affirm (continue) the contract and perhaps claim for damages later.

9.5 Discharge by frustration

- A contract may be discharged by the doctrine of frustration if, after formation and during the life of a contract, events outside the control of either party occur that make performance of the contract illegal, impossible or drastically change the nature of the obligations that were originally contracted for.
- The effect of frustration is an immediate and effective end of the contract at the point when an event occurs preventing performance. Neither party will be obliged to fulfil future obligations.
- This has not always been the case and this area of frustration has developed in three ways. It used to be irrelevant if after a contract's formation it became impossible to perform obligations.

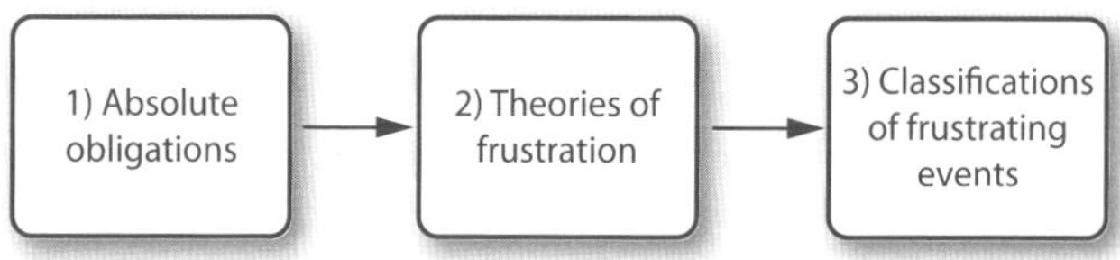

Definition

Absolute obligations: This 'doctrine' provides that responsibilities under a contract are absolute.

9.5.1 Absolute obligations

This was the start of the doctrine of frustration. Despite an event outside their control a party was obliged to perform their obligations or pay damages.

Case:	
***Paradine v Jane* (1647)**	Despite land being occupied for three years during the English Civil War, Jane was still obliged to pay the rent owed to Paradine.

9.5.2 Theories of frustration

There are two theories behind the development away from the doctrine of 'absolute obligations' to the doctrine of frustration.

Research Point

Can the doctrine of frustration apply to a lease of land?

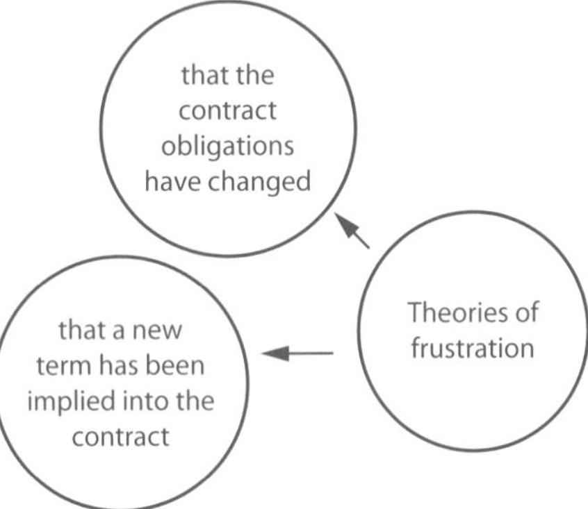

- Implied terms theory – the case of *Taylor v Caldwell* (1863) at the Court of the Queen's Bench was crucial to the development of the doctrine of frustration, with judges in the nineteenth century recognising the limitations of the doctrine of absolute obligations.

Case:	
***Taylor v Caldwell* (1863)**	Facts: Caldwell agreed to rent a concert hall to Taylor. After the signing of the contract but before any performance the hall was destroyed by fire, which was no fault of either party. There was no contractual reference to such a scenario. Taylor relied on the doctrine of absolute obligations since he had spent large sums of money on advertising and marketing and sued for breach of contract. Held: The court in excusing both sides from future contractual responsibilities turned down the claim. Blackburn J said that the contract was subject to an implied term that the concert hall would remain in existence until fulfilment of the contract was due: *'in contracts where performance depends on the continued existence of a given person or thing, a condition is implied that the impossibility of performance arising from the perishing of the person or thing shall excuse the performance. In none of these cases is the promise in words other than positive, nor is there any express stipulation that the destruction of the person or thing shall excuse the performance; but that excuse is by law implied because from the nature of the contract it is apparent that the parties contracted on the basis of the continued existence of the particular person or chattel'.*

Workpoint

It is right to call into question the idea that the implied term theory rests on fiction?

- A change in the obligations – there was a shift away from the implied term theory with its basis becoming questionable. Lord Radcliffe in *Davies Contractors Ltd v Fareham UDC* (1956) stated:

'there is something of a logical difficulty in seeing how the parties could even impliedly have provided for something which ex hypothesi they neither expected nor foresaw; and the ascription of frustration to an implied term of the contract has been criticised as obscuring the true action of the court which consists in applying an objective rule of the law of contract to the contractual obligations that the parties have imposed upon themselves.'

A preferred position said that the contract will be discharged if the parties perform something completely different from that which was contracted for. Lord Radcliffe set out the test thus:

'... there must be a change in the significance of the obligation that the thing undertaken would, if performed, be a different thing than that contracted for.'

Definition

Force majeure clause: A contractual provision providing for what may happen should an unexpected or uncontrollable frustrating event occur.

9.5.3 Classifications of frustrating events

The doctrine of frustration has developed out of the above case law operating in varied scenarios. A contract may become frustrated in three main situations:

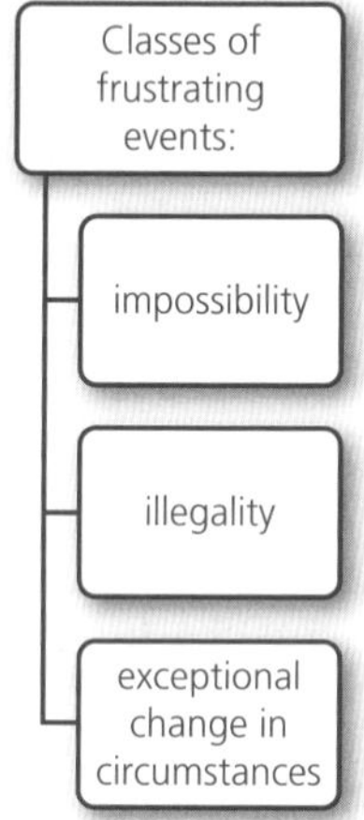

- *Impossibility* – There are a series of events which may lead to the performance of a contract becoming impossible.

Frustrating event	Case
The subject matter of the contract is destroyed – a contract will be frustrated if at the time of performance the subject matter is no longer in existence.	*Taylor v Caldwell* (1863)
The subject matter of the contract is unavailable – a contract will be frustrated if at the time of performance the subject matter is no longer in existence.	*Jackson v Union Marine Insurance Co. Ltd* (1874)
A party is unable to perform their obligations through illness	*Robinson v Davidson* (1871) *Condor v Barron Knights* (1966)
A party is unable to perform their obligations owing to another relevant reason – Any good reason may lead to frustration such as death or length of time a party is unavailable.	*Morgan v Manser* (1948)
An excessive and unavoidable delay – a contract is frustrated where performance has not occurred within a reasonable time due to a prolonged and unavoidable delay in performance.	*Pioneer Shipping Ltd v BTP Toxide Ltd (The Nema)* (1981)

Research Point

What effect has case law had on the development of the doctrine of frustration?

- *Illegality* – A contract will become frustrated where there is a change in the law and further performance would be illegal. The courts will not expect performance where a contract would be performed that is against the law.

An example is the outbreak of war rendering a contract illegal.

Case:	
***Fibrosa SA v Fairburn Lawson Combe Barbour Ltd* (1943)**	A contract was frustrated where a Polish company had contracted with an English company for the acquisition of machinery after the declaration of war owing to Germany's invasion of Poland.

Research Point

Can the taking of property by the government lead to frustration? Consider *Metropolitan Water Board v Dick, Kerr & Co.* (1918) and *FA Tamplin Steamship Co. v Anglo – Mexican Petroleum Products Ltd* (1916).

- *Change in circumstances* – Where an event occurs that means the contract loses its commercial viability, the contract may become frustrated regardless of whether its performance is still a possibility.

Case:	
***Krell v Henry* (1903)**	Facts: Henry contracted with Krell for the hire of a room in Pall Mall to watch the coronation of King Edward VII. There was no mention of the intended use of the room in the contract. The defendant refused to pay for the room when the procession was postponed due to the King being ill. Held: The court found the contract had been frustrated: the procession of the King on that date was the foundation of the contract.

Frustration will not occur, however, where the frustrating event does not deny commercial viability in its entirety. This is demonstrated in *Herne Bay Steamboat Co. v Hutton* (1903) which also centres on the coronation of Edward VII.

Case:	
***Herne Bay Steamboat Co. v Hutton* (1903)**	Facts: A ship was hired for two purposes, to see a review of the fleet by the new King and second to sail round the Solent to see the fleet in its entirety (which was not a common occurrence). The court refused the claim of frustration. Held: whilst the purpose of seeing the King's inspection of the fleet could not occur, the purpose of using the boat to see the fleet was still possible and thus not all commercial viability had been lost from the contract. Stirling LJ gave the following opinion: *'The fleet was there, and passengers might have been found willing to go round it. It is true that in the event which happened the object of the voyage became limited, but, in my opinion, that was the risk of the defendant whose venture the taking the passengers was.'*

This position is also reflected in the leasing of land. The rent would still be owed even if, for example, a farm house was destroyed by fire. The tenant would still benefit from the use of the land, for example through farming animals, and thus there is still purpose in the lease (*National Carriers Ltd v Panalpina (Northern) Ltd* (1981)).

Workpoint

Can you think of three frustrating and three non-frustrating events not mentioned in here?

9.5.4 Limitations to the doctrine of frustration

- The courts are reluctant to allow a claim of frustration to unfairly mask a breach of contract and have therefore limited its use as shown in the two cases below:

1. In *Tsakiroglou v Noblee Thori* (1961) Viscount Simmonds said:

   'The doctrine of frustration must be applied within very narrow limits.'

2. Lord Roskill in *Pioneer Shipping v BTP Tioxide* (1982) commented that the doctrine of frustration was:

   'not lightly to be invoked to relieve contracting parties of the normal consequences of imprudent commercial bargains'.

- In agreement with this is a non-exhaustive list of scenarios in which the doctrine of frustration cannot be relied upon:

Scenario	Case
• **Self-induced** frustration	*J Lauritzen AS v Wijsmuller BV (The Super Servant Two)* (1990) If the frustration is a direct result of the actions of a party to the contract the doctrine may not be relied upon as a relief of future obligations.
• The contract has become **more difficult** to perform	*Davis Contractors Ltd v Fareham UDC* (1956) Should obligations remain fundamentally the same the contract will not be considered frustrated because it has become more expensive to perform or less beneficial.
• The supervening risk was **foreseeable**	*Amalgamated Investment & Property Co. Ltd v John Walker & Sons Ltd* (1977) Where a risk or supervening event was or should have been foreseeable by both parties at the time the contract was formed then the contract may not be considered frustrated.
• **Provisions** in the contract made for the frustrating event	*Fibrosa Spolka Akcyjna v Fairbairn Lawson Combe Barbour Ltd (The Fibrosa case)* (1943) Should there be appropriate provisions in the contract for frustration it is logical that a claim of frustration will not succeed.
• The contract expressly provides **undertakings** to perform	*Paradine v Jane* (1647) Where the contract stipulates performance should carry on irrespective of intervening events.

Workpoint

Write a definition of a frustrating event.

• *The common law effect*

According to the doctrine of frustration the contract will be terminated at the point of frustration. The parties will be absolved from **future** obligations but not those that arose **before** the frustrating event. This can be demonstrated on the time line below.

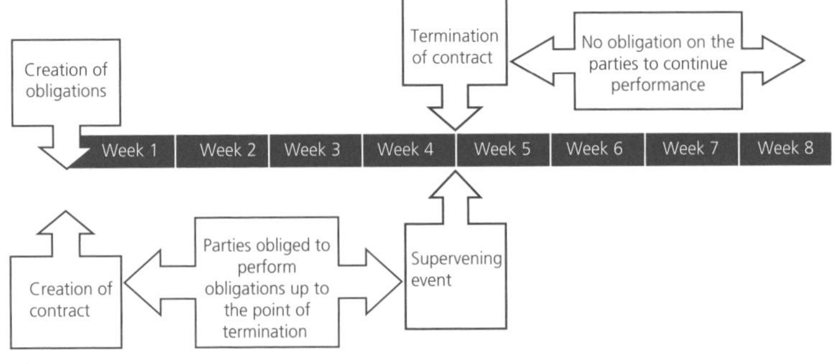

Case:	
***Chandler v Webster* (1904)**	The circumstances again concerned the coronation of King Edward VII and the hiring of a room. In this situation a deposit had been paid with the balance due on the day of the coronation. The claimant pursued a claim for his deposit on the grounds that the contract was frustrated due to the cancellation of the coronation. The claim of frustration was successful but the court prohibited the claimant from recovering the money.

This was considered to be harsh by the House of Lords. They mitigated the common law approach in *Fibrosa Spolka Akcyjna v Fairbairn Lawson Combe Barbour Ltd (The Fibrosa case)*.

Case:	
***Fibrosa Spolka Akcyjna v Fairbairn Lawson Combe Barbour Ltd (The Fibrosa case)* (1943)**	It was held that a party could recover payments made before a frustrating event if there was a total failure of consideration. Lord Macmillan explained: *'Owing to circumstances arising out of present hostilities the contract has become impossible of fulfilment according to its terms. Neither party is to blame. In return for their money the plaintiffs have received nothing whatever from the defendants by way of fulfilment of any part of the contract. It is thus a typical case of total failure of consideration. The money must be repaid.'*

• *The Statutory Effect – Law Reform (Frustrated Contracts) Act 1943*

Whilst *Fibrosa* went some way towards improving the common law position it still demonstrated unfairness in that one party received nothing for work done in advance of the contract.

Mindful of this, Parliament passed the Law Reform (Frustrated Contracts) Act 1943 which applies s 1(1) when:

> *'a contract governed by English law has become impossible of performance or been otherwise frustrated.'*

The Act is concerned with two main areas:

1. Money paid or payable under the contract **s 1(2)**:

   > *'All sums paid or payable to any party in pursuance of the contract before the time when the parties were so discharged (in this Act referred to as 'the time of discharge') shall, in the case of sums so paid, be recoverable from him as money received by him for the use of the party by whom the sums were paid, and, in the case of sums so payable, cease to be so payable:*
   >
   > *Provided that, if the party to whom the sums were so paid or payable incurred expenses before the time of discharge in, or for the purpose of, the performance of the contract, the court may, if it considers it just to do so having regard to all the circumstances of the case, allow him to retain or, as the case may be, recover the whole or any part of the sums so paid or payable, not being an amount in excess of the expenses so incurred.'*

   This supports the decision in *Fibrosa* that consideration money paid in advance is recoverable. The court also has the power to award a 'just sum' in respect of expenses incurred by the payee in their performance of the contract in advance of the contract being discharged (after looking at all the relevant circumstances). An illustration of these rules can be seen in *Gamerco SA v ICM/Fair Warning (Agency) Ltd* (1995).

2. Valuable benefit **s 1(3)**:

   'Where any party to the contract has, by reason of anything done by any other party thereto in, or for the purpose of, the performance of the contract, obtained a valuable benefit (other than a payment of money to which the last foregoing subsection applies) before the time of discharge, there shall be recoverable from him by the said other party such sum (if any), not exceeding the value of the said benefit to the party obtaining it, as the court considers just, having regard to all the circumstances of the case and, in particular —

(a) the amount of any expenses incurred before the time of discharge by the benefited party in, or for the purpose of, the performance of the contract, including any sums paid or payable by him to any other party in pursuance of the contract and retained or recoverable by that party under the last foregoing subsection, and
(b) the effect, in relation to the said benefit, of the circumstances giving rise to the frustration of the contract.'

So there is a two-staged process in the application of s 1(3):

i) There must be a valuable benefit for one party.
ii) The court must decide a just sum not exceeding the benefit in light of the circumstances of the case.

Robert Goff J stated in *BP Exploration Co. (Libya) Ltd v Hunt (No. 2)* (1979) that the overarching theory behind the Act is to prevent the unjust enrichment of a party at the other's expense.

Checkpoint – discharge of contracts

Item on checklist:	Done!
I can state the different ways a contract may be discharged	
I can explain the strict rule and exceptions to the strict rule where a contract is discharged by performance	
I can state how a contract may be discharged through agreement	
I can state the different ways a contract may be discharged by breach	
I can define the doctrine of frustration	
I can explain the theories of frustration	
I can explain the three different classes of frustrating events	
I can state the limitations on the doctrine of frustration	
I can discuss the effects of frustration at common law and the impact of the Law Reform (Frustrated Contracts) Act 1943	

Potential exam questions

1) The doctrine of frustration was developing sufficiently without the need for the Law Reform (Frustrated Contracts) Act 1943.

   Do you agree?

2) Shelly International Air Show takes place every August bank holiday weekend and showcases civilian planes from around the world. Ryan lives next to the end of one of the runways at the air base and lets out his living room every year to people he speaks to on the Shelly Air Show internet forum. In March 2012 he posts a thread on the forum advertising his front room and receives an offer of £1,000 for the use of his room from Jane. Ryan confirms the booking via email and Jane sends him a cheque for £1,000. Consider these scenarios and advise Jane whether she may claim some or all of the £1,000 paid to Ryan:

   a) During the first day of the show a fighter pilot with the Thunder Eagles display team dies when his jet collides with another jet during a display. As a mark of respect the rest of the show is cancelled.

   b) During the first day of the show a fighter pilot with the Thunder Eagles display team dies when his jet collides head-on with another jet during a display. Instead of cancelling the rest of the show, only the Thunder Eagles display team's jets are grounded. All other aeroplanes scheduled to fly do so.

   c) On the morning of the show the UK Government urgently instructs Shelly Air Force Base that due to the sudden outbreak of war, the air force base is only to be used for military operations. The national press believe the war could last some time.

Chapter 10
Remedies

10.1 Introduction

- Remedies are available in the event of different situations occurring in the area of contract law. They include, for example, breach of contract, mistake, misrepresentation and undue influence.
- For cases of breach of contract the usual remedy is damages. This can be claimed as of right by the innocent party and is a **common law** remedy. The aim is to place the party in the position they would have been had the contract been performed.
- Based on the circumstances of the case damages may not be an appropriate form of redress. Therefore an **equitable** remedy may be awarded such as an injunction or specific performance.

10.2 Common law remedies

10.2.1 Damages (unliquidated)

Definition

Damages: A form of financial remedy awarded to a claimant as a result of a breach of contract by the defendant.

- The purpose of damages is to compensate the claimant for financial losses suffered as a result of a breach of contract and place the claimant in the position they would have been had the breach of contract not occurred. Barron Parke in *Robinson v Harman* (1848) stated:

'The rule of the common law is where a party sustains a loss by reason of a breach of contract he is, so far as money can do it, to be placed in the same situation with respect to damages as if the contract had been performed.'

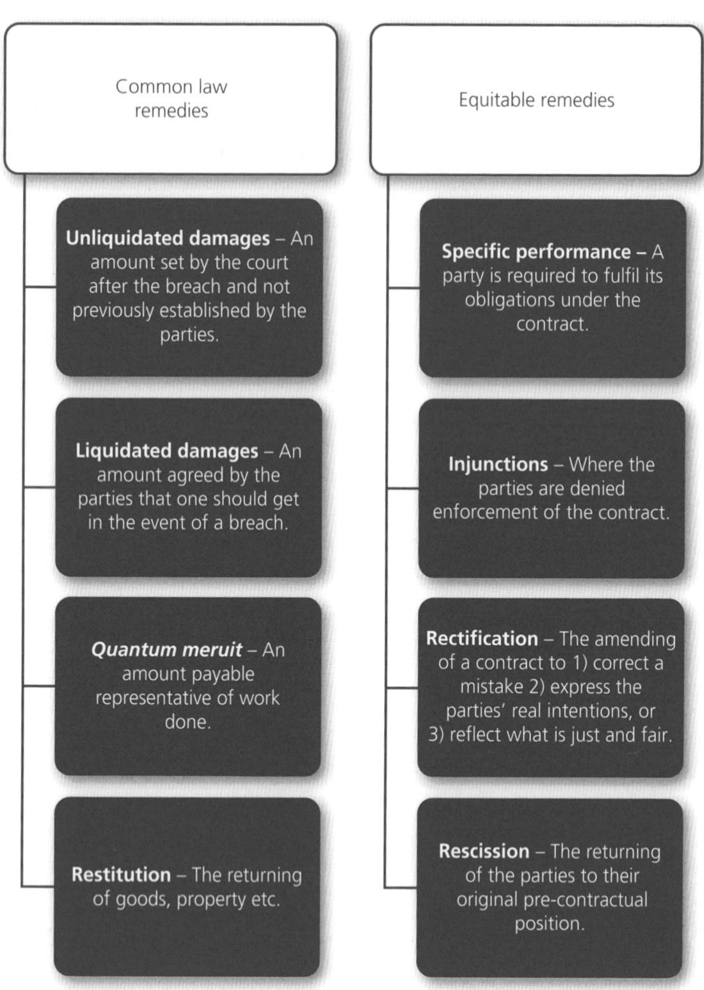

- In *Addis v Gramaphone Co. Ltd* (1909) Lord Atkinson said:

'I have always understood that damages for breach of contract were in the nature of compensation, not punishment.'

- There are things that can limit the availability of damages and these can be categorised as:

  1. causation
  2. remoteness of damage
  3. mitigation of loss.

10.2.2 Causation

- The claimant must be able to show that there is a direct causal link between the loss suffered and the breach of contract by the defendant.
- There must not be a break in the chain of causation. If there is a break in the chain of causation and the intervening act causes the loss then the claimant will not be able to claim damages.
- Should the loss arise as a result of the breach and an intervening event, then providing the chain of causation has not been broken the party in breach of contract may still be liable (*Stansbie v Troman* (1948)).
- Where a breach is part of a sequence of events it may be absolved from being the cause of the loss.

Case:	
***The Monarch SS Co. Case* (1949)**	The owner of a ship was held not liable to a charterer when, as a result of a delay, the ship ran into a typhoon, because such an event could have occurred anywhere.

- The court will decide whether a breach is the main reason for the loss (*London Joint Stock Bank v MacMillan* (1918)) by using a common sense approach (*Galoo Ltd and Others v Bright Grahame Murray* (1995)).

Workpoint

What is the purpose of damages in contract law cases? Do you agree with the purpose?

10.2.3 Remoteness of damage

- It may be the case that not all losses arising from the breach are recoverable. Those losses that are too remote will not be recoverable.
- The principle is referred to as the rule in *Hadley v Baxendale* (1854).

Case:	
Hadley v Baxendale (1854)	The claimants had contracted with the defendants for the delivery of a new crankshaft to replace one that had broken down. The new crankshaft was delivered several days late and thus the defendants were in breach of contract. The defendants were unaware of the crankshaft's importance or that the current crankshaft was broken. As a result the claimants' claim for loss of profit failed. *'Where two parties have made a contract which one of them has broken the damages which the other party ought to receive in respect of such breach of contract should be such as may fairly and reasonably be considered as either arising naturally, ie, according to the usual course of things, from such breach of contract itself, or such as may reasonably be supposed to have been in the contemplation of both parties at the time they made the contract as the probable result of the breach of it.'*

- The requirements of remoteness can be satisfied through two different limbs.

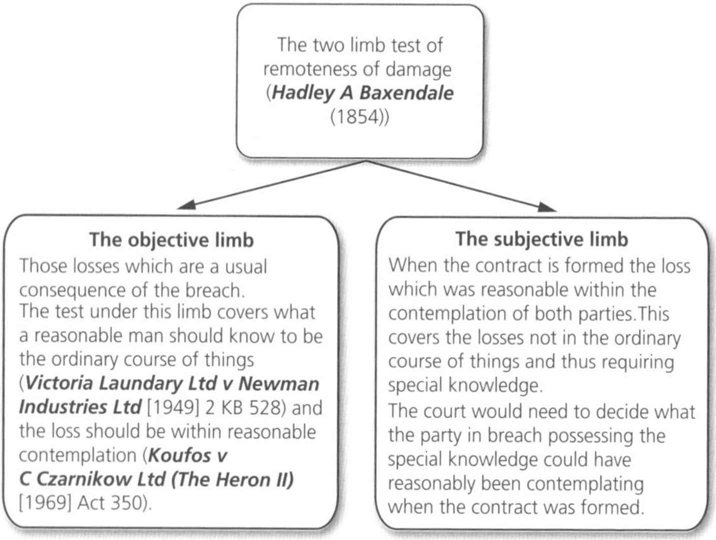

The two limb test of remoteness of damage (***Hadley A Baxendale*** (1854))

The objective limb
Those losses which are a usual consequence of the breach.
The test under this limb covers what a reasonable man should know to be the ordinary course of things (***Victoria Laundary Ltd v Newman Industries Ltd*** [1949] 2 KB 528) and the loss should be within reasonable contemplation (***Koufos v C Czarnikow Ltd (The Heron II)*** [1969] Act 350).

The subjective limb
When the contract is formed the loss which was reasonable within the contemplation of both parties.This covers the losses not in the ordinary course of things and thus requiring special knowledge.
The court would need to decide what the party in breach possessing the special knowledge could have reasonably been contemplating when the contract was formed.

- The Court of Appeal was able to reaffirm the principle in *Victoria Laundry Ltd v Newman Industries Ltd* (1949).

Case:	
***Victoria Laundry Ltd v Newman Industries Ltd* (1949)**	A boiler was not delivered on time. The claimants successfully recovered damages for their usual profits. However they failed in the recovery of losses resulting from their inability to fulfil a government contract since the government contract could not be expected to be in the minds of the defendants when they contracted with the claimants.

Research Point

What were the critical issues made by Asquith LJ on the subject of remoteness in *Victoria Laundry Ltd v Newman Industries Ltd* (1949)?

Research Point

What legal principle did *Wroth v Tyler* (1974) establish? Did *Brown v KMR Services* affirm or reject the principle?

- Clarity was found in *Koufos v C Czarnikow Ltd (The Heron II)* (1969).

Case:	
***Koufos v C Czarnikow Ltd (The Heron II)* (1969)**	Facts: The claimant chartered *The Heron* to deliver sugar. The sugar arrived late by which time the price of sugar had fallen dramatically. The defendant did not know the claimant intended to sell the sugar immediately upon its arrival. Held: The House of Lords allowed the claim for loss of profits under the subjective limb of *Hadley* since the defendant knew he was carrying sugar and the port which it would be delivered to was a popular trading place for sugar. As such it must have been in contemplation when the defendants contracted with the claimants.

- In *Jackson v Royal Bank of Scotland* (2005) the House of Lords considered the matters of remoteness and any limitation on liability in damages. The House of Lords said that the point at which the rule (or test) in *Hadley* may be applied is the point at which the contract is formed not when any breach may have occurred. The court justified their position on the basis that it is at the stage of forming a contract when liability for damages may be limited by a party.

Research Point

Read 'Hadley v Baxendale foreseeability: A principle beyond its sell-by date?', *Journal of Contract Law*, vol. 23, 2007, 120–147.

What are the key issues raised by Professor Tettenborn?

10.2.4 The duty to mitigate

Lastly there is an obligation on any claimant to proceedings to mitigate their loss. There are ultimately three rules to remember:		
1) The claimant cannot recover for loss which could have been avoided had the claimant taken reasonable steps.	2) The claimant cannot recover for any loss he has actually avoided, irrespective of whether he took more steps than were necessary in acquiescence with the above rule.	3) The claimant may recover loss incurred in taking reasonable steps to mitigate his loss, even though he did not succeed.

- The failure of a claimant to mitigate the extent of any loss suffered may have an adverse affect on any award of damages in their favour.
- The principle effectively encourages parties to minimise any losses suffered or likely to be suffered:

'… which impose on a plaintiff the duty of taking all reasonable steps to mitigate the loss consequent on the breach, and debars him from claiming any part of the damage which is due to his neglect to take such steps'. (Lord Haldane in British Westinghouse v Underground Railway Co. *(1912)).*

- However:

'this does not impose on the plaintiff an obligation to take any step which a reasonable and prudent man would not ordinarily take in the course of his business'. (Lord Haldane in British Westinghouse v Underground Railway Co.*).*

Case:	
***Brace v Calder* (1895)**	Facts: The claimant was employed in a managerial role by the defendants for two years. After five months the company was restructured which resulted in the claimant losing his job. The claimant was offered a new role within the company which he declined. The court refused the claimant's claim for damages. Held: The court considered the offer of re-employment was reasonable and by rejecting the offer the claimant was acting unreasonably and thus failing to mitigate his loss.

- A claimant will not be required to go to extraordinary lengths to mitigate their loss. A solicitor, in breach of contract, obtained a house (which had a defective title) for the claimant. The solicitor defended an action brought by the claimant arguing that the claimant ought to have mitigated his loss by suing the vendor under the covenants for title under s 76 Law of Property Act 1925. Harman J remarked:

'The so-called duty to mitigate does not go so far as to oblige the injured party, even under an indemnity, to embark on a complicated and difficult piece of litigation against a third party … it is no part of the plaintiff's duty to embark on the proposed litigation in order to protect his solicitor from the consequences of his own carelessness.'

Definition

Duty to mitigate: An obligation placed on a party to do what is reasonable to minimise its losses.

10.2.5 Damages (liquidated)

- It is possible that the parties may agree on a fixed sum of damages in the event of a breach. This type of clause is referred to as a '**liquidated damages**' clause.
- The parties will be bound by the amount agreed if it accurately reflects the loss suffered. A further or supplementary action for unliquidated damages will not be allowed.
- Should the amount not accurately reflect the loss and if it can be considered a punishment for a breach this will be considered a '**penalty**' clause. In *Bridge v Campbell Discount Co.* (1962) a depreciation clause in a hire-purchase contract for a car was declared void as a penalty as it bore no reflection to the actual depreciation in value.

- Penalty clauses bear no legal significance and a court will disregard them. In such circumstances the innocent party will still be entitled to claim unliquidated damages (*Wall v Rederiaktiebolaget Luggude* (1915)).

The courts will use the test of Lord Dunedin in ***Dunlop Pneumatic Tyre Co. v New Garage and Motor Co.*** [1914] AC79 in deciding whether a liquidated damages clause accuratety reflects the loss suffered. The test contains the following points:

1) An extravagant sum will always be regarded as a penalty	2) It will normally be considered a penalty where there is a payment of a large sum to settle a small debt	3) A fixed sum covering a variety of breaches will ordinarily be considered a breach

Workpoint

What test will the courts use to decide whether a clause is a penalty or legitimate liquidated damages?

10.2.6 Heads of damage and calculation

- A court may make an award for unliquidated damages on the basis of three different assessments.

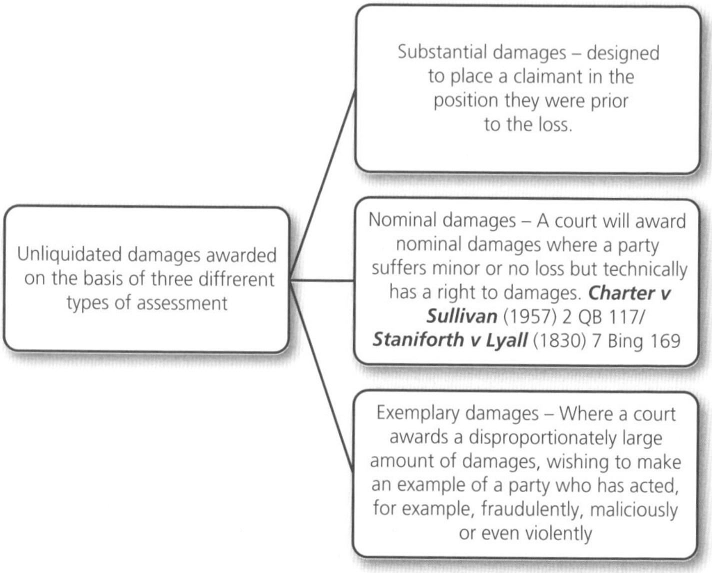

Unliquidated damages awarded on the basis of three diffrerent types of assessment

- Substantial damages – designed to place a claimant in the position they were prior to the loss.
- Nominal damages – A court will award nominal damages where a party suffers minor or no loss but technically has a right to damages. ***Charter v Sullivan*** (1957) 2 QB 117/ ***Staniforth v Lyall*** (1830) 7 Bing 169
- Exemplary damages – Where a court awards a disproportionately large amount of damages, wishing to make an example of a party who has acted, for example, fraudulently, maliciously or even violently

- Damages are available as of right and it should be remembered that before they are calculated they are subject to causation, remoteness and mitigation as discussed above.
- There are other areas that a calculation can be based on. These are:
  - loss of bargain;
  - reliance loss; and
  - restitution.

10.2.7 Loss of bargain

- This aspect of damages aims to place the party in the position they would have been in **had the contract been performed**.
- There are several situations lending themselves to the possibility of the claimant recovering damages under this header as shown in the following table.

Loss of opportunity or profit	The courts have allowed claims for the loss of an opportunity despite such losses inherently being difficult to quantify. The loss of profit may occur where but for the contract not being completed the claimant would have made a profit.	*Chaplin v Hicks* (1911)
Non-performance by one of the parties to the contract	This occurs through the failure to deliver goods, provide a service or accept delivery. Damages are based on a price obtainable in an 'available market' and the actual agreed contract price.	*Charter v Sullivan* (1957)
The **'available market' rule**	A claimant was ordinarily able to claim full losses if there was **no available market** (*W L Thompson Ltd v Robinson Gunmakers Ltd* (1955)). However the rule is not as unyielding as it once was.	*Shearson Lehman Hutton Inc. v Maclaine Watson & Co Ltd (No. 2)* (1990)
The goods or services are defective	The goods or services are defective or the contract requires a better quality of good or service than was actually received. Damages will cover the expense of replacing the goods at the required standard or be based on the reduction in value of the goods.	*Ruxley Electronics and Construction Ltd v Forsyth* (1995)

10.2.8 Reliance loss

- This basis of damage calculation is aimed at placing the claimant in the position they would have been **had the contract never been performed.**

- It may not be possible for a court to quantify the position the parties would have been in if the contract was performed. As a result the court's basis for calculation could be placed on the loss caused by reliance on the contract.

Case:	
***Anglia Television Ltd v Reed* (1972)**	The claimant contracted with the defendant for him to play a lead role in their film. He breached the contract by pulling out of production before the film was completed. The court was not able to predict how well the film would have done or the subsequent profits and in essence the position the claimants would have been in had the contract been performed (loss of expectation). The court was, however, able to quantify the expenditure of the claimants before the contract's formation and thus awarded damages on the position the claimants would have been in had they not entered into the contract (or the loss caused by reliance on the contract).

- The decision rests with the claimant whether she claims damages for the loss of expectation or the loss caused by reliance on the contract's performance.

Workpoint

Tom has bought a painting for £500 from an antique dealer friend. The painting is actually worth £750, but when he gets home he notices a crack in the frame which means the painting is only worth £375. What could Tom's reliance loss be?

10.2.9 Restitutionary loss

- Restitutionary damages aim to give back to the claimant the value of any benefit the defendant may have received owing to unjust enrichment.

- This form of damages is a 'last resort' and will be awarded where the reliance or expectation loss cannot be protected. The suitability of the reward may be determined by the consideration or lack of it (*Stocznia Gdanska SA v Latvian Shipping Co.* (1998)).

Workpoint

What are the facts and legal principle of *Attorney General v Blake* (2001)?

10.2.10 Non-pecuniary loss and cases of 'mental distress'

- In contract law the courts are much more at ease in awarding damages for exact or precise pecuniary losses. Formerly 'mental distress', injury to feelings and so on would not constitute an award of damages, as can be seen in *Addis v The Gramophone Company* (1909) and *Hurst v Picture Theatres* (1915). However the situation has since been modified through case law developments so that where there is injury to feelings, loss of amenity or 'mental distress' damages will be recoverable.
- An exception to the rule can be found in what became known as the 'holiday cases' such as *Cook v Spanish Holidays* (1960) and *Jarvis v Swan Tours Ltd* (1973) where peace of mind was central to the contract.

Case:	
Cook v Spanish Holidays **(1960)**	A newly married couple who were on their honeymoon were awarded damages when the hotel company made a double-booking leaving the honeymooners without a room on their wedding night.
Jarvis v Swan Tours Ltd **(1973)**	The claimant had his award of damages increased on appeal. The court held that the very purpose of the holiday was enjoyment and as such the damages should reflect this where the level of enjoyment promised had fallen so far short.

- In *Diesen v Sampson* (1971) damages were awarded to reflect the displeasure and upset caused when a wedding photographer failed to show up. A court awarded damages when a solicitor in *Heywood v Wellers* (1976) caused the claimant mental distress when he failed to get an injunction protecting the claimant from molestation. However, the rule must nevertheless have boundaries (*Hayes v James and Charles Dodd* (1990)).

- Where the contract's sole purpose is the provision of a pleasurable amenity, loss of such an amenity may bring an award of damages.

Case:	
***Ruxley Electronics and Construction Ltd v Forsyth* (1995)**	The House of Lords awarded loss of amenity damages when the claimant's swimming pool was made to the wrong specifications and therefore affected his pleasure of diving into the pool.

- The development of case law in this area of contract law can be seen in the timeline below.

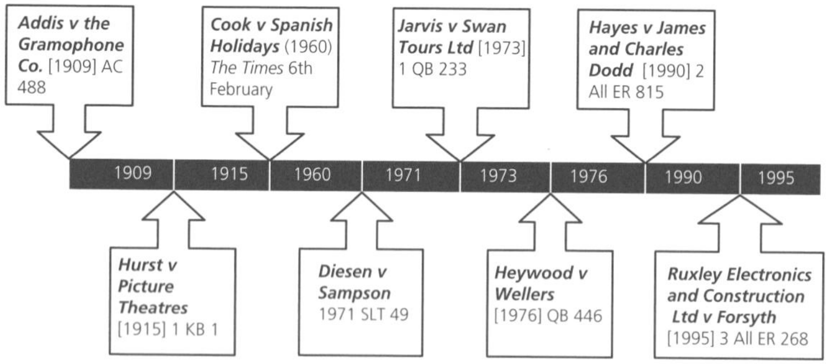

Research Point

Read the paper *Aggravated, Exemplary and Restitutionary Damages* (1993) (Law Com. No. 132) and summarise its key points.

Workpoint

What is the purpose of damages based on:

1) loss of bargain?

2) reliance loss?

3) restitutionary loss?

10.2.11 *Quantum meruit* claims

- A claim for *quantum meruit* is a claim for work done: an amount of money that reflects the part-performance of the contract. An example can be found in *Planche v Colburn* (1831). The claimant had written a book as part of a series. The whole series was abandoned and despite having worked extensively on the book the author was unable to finish it. The court allowed him to claim half his fee for the work he had done.

10.3 Equitable remedies

10.3.1 Introduction

- The common law remedy of damages is available once there is a breach of contract ('as of right'). Equitable remedies are awarded at the discretion of the court. Equitable remedies will be available where damages are not appropriate.
- Examples of where damages would not reflect the needs of the claimant include:

1. where the subject matter is unique and no other equivalent could be purchased;
2. the defendant is unable to pay the damages or they are unquantifiable;
3. a party entered the contract under a misrepresentation or mistake.

- Equitable remedies that may be used in such circumstances include:
  - specific performance
  - injunctions
  - rescission
  - rectification.

10.3.2 Specific performance

- This is where the court orders a party to fulfil their obligations under the contract. A party is required to fulfil their obligations and the remedy is therefore **positive** in nature. Contrast this with an injunction which is preventative and thus prevents a party from doing something.
- In deciding whether to grant specific performance as a remedy the court will consider several rules:

- *Not available where damages would be an adequate remedy* – like injunctions, should damages be an appropriate form of remedy specific performance will not be granted, *Wroth v Tyler* (1974).
- *There must be mutuality* – the remedy must be available to both parties should the roles and circumstances be reversed (*Flight v Bolland* (1828)).
- *The granting of specific performance must be equitable* – if it is inequitable the court will not grant the remedy.

Case:	
***Patel v Ali* (1984)**	The Court of Appeal refused to allow specific performance. The vendor was disabled and reliant on others. Forcing her to move would have created undue hardship.

- *Specific performance must be claimed without undue delay* – Specific performance may not be claimed where there has been a significant delay in doing so. 'Delay defeats equity'; however what constitutes a delay significant enough to defeat equity is a matter for the courts to decide.
- *Specific performance is not available in contracts of employment or contracts for personal services* – the court will not force someone to work for an employer. It is both unconscionable and inequitable.
- *Court supervision of the specific performance must not be required* – specific performance will not be granted as a remedy if the court would have to persistently monitor the parties to ensure they are complying with the order. In *Ryan v Mutual Tontine Westminster Chambers Association* (1893) the tenancy agreement stated that the landlord was to provide a porter to be working all the time. Specific performance was not granted by the court since it was unable to constantly supervise the situation.

Research Point

What effect does the Trade Union and Labour Relations (Consolidation) Act 1992 have on contracts for personal services?

10.3.3 Injunctions

- An injunction is an equitable remedy that may prevent a party from acting in breach of contract. An injunction may be **mandatory** or **prohibitory**.

Mandatory injunction

- This requires a party to the contract to make a positive act, usually rectifying the breach of contract. An example can be seen in *Wakeham v Wood* (1981) where the court awarded a mandatory injunction to pull down a house after the defendant had built on land in breach of a restrictive covenant.

Prohibitory injunction

- Will be granted by the court to prevent a party from doing something. It is widely considered that an injunction will not be approved if the outcome is to directly or indirectly force the defendant to do something which the claimant could not have been required to do by specific performance, for example to require performance of a contract for personal services (*Page One Records v Britton* (1968)).
- The courts will only grant the injunction if the contract expressly states that a defendant is prohibited from doing a particular act.

Case:	
***Lumley v Wagner* (1852)**	The defendant had a three-month contract and as part of that contract it was expressly stated she would not work with another theatre. Whilst under contract she agreed to work for another theatre at the same time. An injunction was successfully sought to prevent her from performing her second contract. It should be noted that she was not therefore being compelled to work for the claimants, because she could do other work to earn a living.

- The decision in *Lumley* was followed in *Warner Bros Inc. v Nelson* (1937) where the claimants succeeded in a request for an injunction preventing the actress Bette Davis from taking alternative employment.

Research Point

Why might the granting of injunctions in *Lumley v Wagner* (1852) and *Warner Bros Inc. v Nelson* (1937) be criticised?

10.3.4 Rescission

- The remedy of rescission aims to put the parties back into their previous positions, as they were before the contract's formation.
- Where a contract has been set aside a party will be entitled to avoid the contract and any of its obligations and responsibilities. A contract may also be set aside where one of the parties would not have contracted had it been aware of the misrepresentation or mistake prior to the contract's formation.
- Rescission is covered in detail in the chapter in this book on misrepresentation. The table below summarises the conditions upon which a decision to rescind would be decided by the court.

'restitutio in integrum'	It must be possible to return the parties to their original position before the contract was formed. *Clarke v Dickson* (1858)
A third party has acquired rights	Where a third party has honestly acquired rights in the subject matter an action for rescission will be unsuccessful. *Oakes v Turquand and Harding* (1867)
'Delay defeats equity'	As with other remedies in equity, should a party seek rescission after an excessive delay the court will be reluctant to grant the request. *Leaf v International Galleries* (1950)
The contract must not have been affirmed	A court will not allow rescission if the claimant has acted in a way to affirm the contract. *Long v Lloyd* (1958)

10.3.5 Rectification

- Where the parties to a contract hold an agreement which is not accurately reflected in a written contract, the court may exercise its discretion to amend the written contract to reflect the true agreement of the parties. The written agreement must be contrary to the actual agreement between the parties.

Case:	
***Craddock Bros Ltd v Hunt* (1923)**	The claimant successfully sought rectification when a yard was wrongly included in the sale of a house.

Workpoint

Summarise the range of equitable remedies available in contract law and when they may be used.

Checkpoint – remedies

Item on checklist:	**Done!**
I can discuss the two major types of remedy	
I can define the two limbed test of remoteness of damage (*Hadley v Baxendale* (1854))	
I can explain the requirements to successfully prove the different types of mistake	
I can explain the three rules appropriate when a party is obliged to mitigate their loss	
I can explain the significance of *Dunlop Pneumatic Tyre Co. v New Garage and Motor Co.* (1914)	
I know the three different types of unliquidated damages	
I can define loss of bargain, reliance loss, restitutionary loss, non-pecuniary loss and cases of 'mental distress'	
I can explain when a equitable remedy may be appropriate	

Potential exam questions

'Damages are an effective remedy for breach of contract.' To what extent do you agree with this statement?

Glossary

Absolute obligations This 'doctrine' provides that responsibilities under a contract are absolute.
Acceptance The communication of an unequivocal and unconditional agreement to a valid offer.
Affirm 'To carry on with'. Where A seeks to have a contract with B affirmed, A seeks to carry on the contract with B.
Anticipatory breach This is a statement by one of the parties to the contract that they do not intend to complete some or all of their obligations or responsibilities under the contract. This may be implied by conduct.
Assumpsit A common law form of action allowing a party relief for a breach of contract or a breach of an informal promise.
Bilateral discharge Both parties gain from the new agreement to discharge.
Caveat emptor Let the buyer beware.
Consensus ad idem A 'meeting of minds' where both parties have the same understanding of the terms of a contract.
Consideration The price paid by one party for the other party's promise.
Contra preferentem A rule stating that an exemption clause is interpreted against the party that inserted it into the contract and seeks to rely upon it.
Contract 'A contract is an agreement giving rise to obligations which are enforced or recognised by law. The factor which distinguishes contractual from other legal obligations is that they are based on the agreement of the contracting parties.' (Sir Guenter Treitel *The Law of Contract* (12th edition, Sweet & Maxwell, 2007).
Counter-offer The changing of an important term or the suggestion of an alternative set of terms by the offeree.
Damages A form of financial remedy awarded to a claimant as a result of a breach of contract by the defendant.
De minimis non curat lex The law does not concern itself with trifles or microscopic deviations.
Dealing as a consumer S 12 says that a party will be dealing as a consumer if they do not make the contract in the course of business nor pretend to do so.
Detinue An action for deliverance of a chattel.
Duress Where a party is induced to enter a contract by violence or threats of violence.
Duty to mitigate An obligation placed on a party to do what is reasonable to minimise its losses.
Economic duress The forcing of contract variation by one party in a commercial contract through the use of coercion or commercial pressure.
Estoppel The barring or denying of a party from affirming a particular claim

(or fact) inconsistent with a previous position that a party took, through words or conduct, especially where a representation has been acted or relied upon by others.

Exclusion clause Where a party is entitled to exclude their liability.

Executed consideration This occurs where one party has 'executed' or 'carried out' their side of the bargain. The other party's consideration is pending completion and thus executory.

Executory consideration Concerns an agreement to carry out an act in the future.

***Force majeure* clause** A contractual provision providing for what may happen should an unexpected or uncontrollable frustrating event occur.

Fundamental breach This is also known as a **repudiatory** breach of contract. It is so serious that it allows the innocent party to terminate performance of the contract and pursue a claim for damages.

Honourable pledge clause A clause contained within a contract stipulating the contract has no legal basis and cannot be enforced. *Rose and Frank Co. v J R Crompton and Bros* (1925).

'In the course of business' The decision in *R and B Customs Brokers Co. Ltd v United Dominions Trust Ltd* means the transaction must be an essential part of the business.

Invitation to treat To invite an offer. An expression of willingness to negotiate.

Letter of comfort A letter by a party to a contact to another party stating an eagerness to enter into contractual obligations without the rudiments of a legally enforceable contract. *Kleinwort Benson Ltd v Malaysia Mining Corporation Bhd* (1989).

Limitation clause The restriction of a party's liability.

Misrepresentation: A false statement of fact that persuades another party to enter into a contract.

Mutual mistake Both parties have made different mistakes and are at cross-purposes.

Nemo dat quod non habet No one may transfer ownership of something they do not own.

Non est factum A mistake in respect of a written agreement.

The objective principle 'A person's words or conduct must be interpreted in the manner in which another might objectively and reasonably understand them.' (Lord Steyn, 'Contract Law: Fulfilling the Reasonable Expectations of Honest Men' (1997) 113 LQR 433)

Offer An expression of willingness by the offeror to contract on a set of specific terms and/or conditions with the intention to be bound by the contract once the offer is accepted.

Offeree A person, group, organisation receiving the offer.

Offeror The person, group, organisation making the offer.

Parol evidence rule Oral and/or intrinsic evidence is not admissable to add, vary or contradict a written contract.
Prima facie On first appearance.
Privity of contract In order to sue or be sued in contract law a person or business must be privy (a party) to that contract.
Quantum meruit Payment for the work done. Latin: 'as much as is deserved'.
Representations Statements made at the pre-contractual stage.
Res extincta A mistake as to the subject matter's **existence.**
Res sua A mistake as to the subject matter's **ownership.**
Rescission Setting the contract aside.
Restitutio in integrum Restoration to the original position.
Revocation Withdrawal of an offer.
Subject to contract An agreement that is not legally effective as a contract.
Uberrimae fidei Of utmost good faith.
Undue influence Where a party is induced to enter a contract by improper and unfair pressure.
Unilateral discharge One party releases the other from their obligations and therefore one party benefits from the discharge.
Unilateral mistake One party to the contract is mistaken and the other party is aware, or the circumstances suggest they should be aware, of the mistake.

Index